Crumbling Dreams: What You Must Know Before Building or Buying a New House (or Condo)

Ruth S. Martin, M.D.

Crumbling Dreams: What You Must Know Before Building or Buying a New House (or Condo)

Publisher's Cataloging in Publication
(Prepared by Quality Books, Inc.)

Martin, Ruth S., 1946-
    Crumbling dreams: what you must know before building or buying a new house (or condo)/ Ruth S. Martin.
    p. cm.
    Includes bibliographical references and index.
    Preassigned LCCN: 92-072164
    ISBN 1-879653-06-0

    1. House buying. 2. House construction. 3. Home ownership.
I. Title

TH4817.5.M36 1992   643.12
                                   QBI92-1124

DISCLAIMER

My purpose in writing this book is to help anyone buying, or even contemplating buying, a newly-built home. In doing so I pull no punches but "tell it like it is." What I offer are prudent recommendations and sound advice about how to protect yourself when building or buying a new house or condominium. I disclaim liability for any direct or indirect loss or damage that may result from reading this book. Throughout the book I recommend you hire top flight professionals to help investigate and complete your purchase; in fact, that is the only way that you can come close to being fully protected. No book can substitute for professional, local help. The key is to find the "right" people for your house.

If I have made any factual errors, or misquoted any article or person, please let me know. If any reader disagrees with my opinions or recommendations strongly enough to write, I would like to hear from him or her.

Ruth S. Martin, M.D.
Cleveland

FORWARD

In October 1991 I was privileged to testify before the U.S. House of Representatives Subcommittee on Housing and Community Development. The subject was homeowner warranties on new construction. I was invited as head of the non-profit Ridgemere Institute, an organization founded to help homebuyers deal with these 10-year warranties.

In the late 1980s my husband and I bought a new Tennessee home guaranteed by one of the large home warranty companies. After moving in we discovered that our home had been built with major structural defects. Then we learned that the warranty company wasn't going to fix our house's problems without a fight. To make a long story short, I fought a difficult, emotionally-taxing battle. Eventually, we got the company to fulfill it's contractual obligation and pay to fix our house.

Unlike Dr. Martin, we were able to avoid going to trial. Like Dr. Martin, we learned the hard way that the buyer of a defective new house is, with rare exception, unprotected by our civil laws. Our legal system requires buyers of defective construction to expend an enormous amount of time and money to enforce a contract, and the courts do not recognize either expenditure. Equally punishing is the emotional toll. Dr. Martin and others frequently use the word "nightmare" to describe their experiences with a defective new house or condominium. They really mean "pain and suffering," something else not recognized by the courts when you litigate over a defective home.

By chronicling her own story and highlighting numerous other cases of defective construction, Dr. Martin has done you, the reader, a valuable service. I know of no other book that reveals both the many problems that can occur when you build or buy a new home *and* how to prevent them.

Is she qualified to write such a book? Absolutely. Buy a defective house that the responsible people won't fix, and you learn fast. Unfortunately, it is an expensive and not very pleasant education.

Chairman Gonzalez*: Well, thank you very much. You say you're not a lawyer or an engineer?

FORWARD (continued)

Mrs. Fisher: Well, let me tell you, Mr. Chairman, when you start working with these 10-year home protection plans, you learn fast. I now have a Black's Law Dictionary, because they used words I did not understand. It's a very unpleasant experience, but I think if I ever wanted to get a job as a code inspector, I probably could.

Yes, buy a defective house and you too will learn fast. Mainly about what you should have done but didn't. My advice to you: learn before it's too late. *Crumbling Dreams* shows how you, the buyer of new construction, can end up with a well-built, almost headache-free house. For that information alone, the book is worth many times its cover price.

But I hope the book also reaches a more specialized audience: the men and women who make our laws. Dr. Martin's Section 5, "Some advice...," should be entered into the Congressional Record, and read into the minutes of our state legislatures and local governments. She is not a lawyer and I am not a lawyer. But you don't have to be a lawyer to know that, in the realm of new homes and defective construction, existing laws offer no meaningful protection.

Our legislative branches of government need to enact laws to protect us, the people, in our most important purchase: a new home. As things stand now, you have more legal protection when buying a new dishwasher than a new house. As Dr. Martin says, when buying a new house it is still *caveat emptor* — buyer beware — all the way.

Mrs. R. Jean Fisher
Founder, The Ridgemere Institute

------

* U.S. Rep. Henry Gonzalez, Texas, Chairman of the Subcommittee on Housing and Community Development of the Committee on Banking, Finance and Urban Affairs. October 22, 1991. U.S. House of Representatives. Serial No. 102-78, page 28.

Dedicated:

To new-home buyers everywhere,
especially those who received less than they
paid for

Crumbling Dreams: What You Must Know Before Building or Buying a New House (or Condo)

Ruth S. Martin, M.D.

TABLE OF CONTENTS

TABLE OF CONTENTS (continued)

Overview. What you must know before building or buying a new house (or condo)

If you are ever in the position of building or buying a new house or condominium, this book could save you a fortune. And perhaps your sanity as well.

- A couple in North Carolina bought a lot and hired a builder to construct the home of their dreams. One-third way through construction they discovered the foundation was defective. Independent engineering reports came to one conclusion: the structure had to be torn down and the house started all over again. Otherwise, the house would not be safe to live in when completed. The builder denied the extent of the problem. The couple sued him for breach of contract. The builder countersued the couple for work that was not paid for. At the time the lawsuits were filed the couple was out of pocket $130,000.

- After moving into a brand new three story home a Virginia couple discovered serious structural defects. Engineering surveys revealed that the foundation had been built for only a single story home, and that the front of the house was in danger of collapsing. The home warranty company, which guaranteed the structural integrity of the dwelling, refused to make proper repairs. The couple sued. Ultimately, after tremendous aggravation and expense, a Virginia federal appeals court upheld a $206,605 award for the cost of repairs. The couple *lost* $100,000 in unreimbursed legal and experts' fees.

- A couple from Illinois moved into a new house built as part of a subdivision adjacent to a golf course. The house was sited improperly on its lot, and as a result the first floor floods with every heavy rain. Professionals who designed and

1

built the house denied responsibility for the problem. The couple and their two small children can only live in one-half of their house — the top floor. The litigation has already cost them tens of thousands of dollars.

- In the Miami area individual townhomes were built as part of a condominium complex. Most of the homes were guaranteed against structural defects by a large home warranty company. Because of numerous defects found after purchase, county investigators came to inspect the homes and discovered evidence of defective construction. Specifically, they were not built according to local building codes, and were unable to withstand hurricane force winds, a South Florida requirement. The owners were ordered to make the necessary costly repairs or *their homes would be demolished.* Both the builder and warranty company refused to fix the dwellings. A protracted and costly legal battle ensued. The case was settled only after extensive publicity and the involvement of several congressmen.

These are not rare cases of defective construction. In Section 2 you will find many more examples, from all over the country. It's a fact that a small but significant percentage of new-home buyers end up not with the house of their dreams but a lemon: a dwelling constructed with serious defects. Not minor headaches such as scratched floors, broken tiles or loose caulking, but major structural problems like: a foundation that sags because of inadequate landfill; incomplete or improperly placed footers; undersized steel support beams; weak joists underneath the floors; crooked interior walls; peeling exterior framing; crumbling brick veneer; or a roof that acts like a giant sieve when it rains.

Serious defects, usually structural in nature, are often hard to spot before you live in the house. Occasionally the defects show up before the house is completed, as happened to the North Carolina couple. More often they show up within a year after you move in, although sometimes they take several years to uncover. One famous media star ended up suing contractors over his defective $4.5 million California home *six years* after it was built.

A serious defect is easy to define. It is one that will a) be very costly to repair and b) make your house or condo unsalable until fixed. Discover a serious defect anytime after you move in and, in all likelihood, you can kiss your home equity goodbye. At least until the problem is fully repaired which, as you'll see, can take years.

Buy a house with serious defects and you are at risk for a nightmare beyond belief. I know, because it happened to me and my family. I am a psychiatrist and my husband is also a physician, and we have three children. What ensued after we discovered that our custom-built house was full of defects proved so dramatic and traumatizing I wrote a book about the experience, from contract to lawsuit to trial (*And They Built A Crooked House*, Lakeside Press, Cleveland; see page 171).

Long before the book was published we learned that our house misfortune was not unique. Similar nightmares have happened — and continue to happen — to many naive new-home buyers. Like the North Carolinian who discovered, among many other structural defects in his new $212,000 home, that the "bricks used to construct the perimeter foundation. . .were void of mortar."

No one knows how many buyers get stuck with a lemon, but if only 3% of new construction comes with serious defects — a low estimate — that represents over 30,000 new houses in a recession year and 60,000 houses in boom times. You don't want to end up owning one of them.

Whatever the exact number of new homes sold with major defects, you are probably unaware of the problem. Unlike another major consumer headache, defective cars, there is usually little or no publicity about construction defects. Many homeowners actually fear publicity, lest it damage the resale value of their home if and when the defects are repaired. Also limiting publicity is the fact that there is no General Motors, Ford or Chrysler of the housing industry, so construction problems and complaints don't focus on a few national companies.

In stark contrast with autos, the housing industry is intensely local. Thousands of individual builders are responsible for the over one million new houses sold each year in the U.S. The local nature of house construction means that stories about defective houses, unhappy home buyers and lawsuits against builders tend to stay local. This is true even if several defective homes are built in one location by a company that does business in other states. Since construction is on-site instead of in a factory, newspapers tend to assume that a Floridian's defective house problems, for example, are of no concern to Californians, Ohioans or New Yorkers.

In fact, construction defects and the nightmarish legal consequences that occur in any one area should concern new-home buyers wherever they live. If every construction horror story that made local headlines was entered into a data base and publicized state by state, new-home buyers would be astounded at the magnitude of the problem.

Response to my first book, from all over the country, has made me aware of how often people are victimized by shoddy construction. Legislators are beginning to pay attention. In October 1991 Congress held hearings on defective construction that carries federally-guaranteed mortgages. Also in 1991, the North Carolina legislature passed a bill to provide homeowners the money to fix a defective new house, providing the homeowners: a) have sued the builder in court, b) obtained a legal judgment *and*, c) the builder has declared bankruptcy (a common situation with builders who are sued). Unfortunately the North Carolina bill does not ensure reimbursement for legal expenses — an amount which often exceeds the cost of repairs!

Reader response has also taught me something else. Although houses are constructed locally by thousands of individual contractors, when serious defects occur and the builder won't fix them the outcome is always the same for the homeowners: *they are trapped.* They cannot repair the house without spending thousands of dollars extra, they cannot force the builder to fix it and they cannot sell it. Whether or not the victims choose to fight a legal battle, the situation invariably leads to major stress, wasted hours too numerous to count and a significant financial loss. A true *nightmare.*

Why is this invariably the situation? One reason is the absence of laws to protect you after the fact, that is, after you have closed the deal on a defective house. Unlike lemon laws for autos, no state has enacted laws to make builders fix major mistakes or buy back a seriously-defective house. Every state has laws regarding contract obligations and the like, but they are not written to protect the buyer of a structurally-defective house or condo. In truth, the consumer has more protection when buying a refrigerator or new car than a new home. This assertion is based on many, many situations where home buyers thought they were protected by contracts, guarantees and promises but, much to their horror, were not.

What about your community's occupancy permit, the document that grants you the right to move in to your new house? This permit provides no protection against serious defects; it certainly does not guarantee the house's structural integrity, nor does it even purport to. Even when inspectors miss major defects — and the house is not built in accordance with local building codes — the community is protected from lawsuit by the doctrine of 'sovereign immunity.' You cannot pursue a legal battle against the inspectors or the municipality, no matter what is wrong with your house.

What if you have a builder's guarantee or a homeowner's warranty? As you'll see, these become mere pieces of paper if the builder or insurer doesn't stand behind them. "Stand behind" means they are willing — without the threat of legal action — to recognize serious defects *and* fix them. Far more often than potential new-home buyers realize, the responsible people *don't* stand behind their promises, their contractual guarantees, their written warranties. This book will show you why.

What about hiring a lawyer to draw up a contract with the builder or developer before you take possession of a new house? Won't a contract from your own lawyer, signed by the builder, protect you? No, not if the builder reneges. In fact a contract with an irresponsible builder may be worse than none at all, for not only do you pay extra dollars for the document but it will cost you thousands more to try to enforce. And you will *never* recoup your expenses.

What if your lawyer says not to worry, that the law is on your side? Worry. Any lawyer worth his (or her) salt will tell you what we heard repeatedly during our long ordeal: "a contract is only as good as the people behind it." Despite whatever laws may exist in your state, any attempt to enforce a contract against irresponsible people will be a litigation nightmare. It will cost you time, money and peace of mind. You and your family will lose no matter what the legal outcome. Don't forget it is you, not your lawyer, who become the victim when people building or insuring your house don't stand behind their promises.

If you buy a new house of condo with serious defects and the responsible people can't or won't fix them, you are in trouble no matter what assurances have been made, no matter what contracts or guarantees have been signed, no matter what laws exist in your state. You will find yourself out of luck, not to mention out of a whole bundle of money. *Crumbling Dreams* not only shows why this is so, but tells how to prevent the ultimate consumer nightmare: a seriously defective new house or condo.

*　　*　　*

Crumbling Dreams is not an anti-builder book. Nor is it anti-developer, anti-architect, anti-lawyer or even anti-new houses. It is a profoundly pro-consumer book, a book unlike any other you will find on the subject of buying or building a new house. I can make this statement because I've reviewed practically every book on the subject; many of them are listed in the Bibliography. Each of these books has something useful to offer, although none spells out the legal, financial and emotional consequences of buying a defectively-constructed house.

This book will open your eyes to the worst that can happen with your new house or condominium — and the worst is what you should be concerned about. Knowing what could happen if you are not careful, and taking a few simple steps before you sign on the dotted line, can mean the difference between realized dreams and crumbling dreams. To help protect the value and integrity of your new home, read this book. It could save you a fortune.

SECTION 1. And They Built a Crooked House: How one couple lost a fortune while winning the largest residential construction case ever tried in their state

Section 1 is a synopsis of my first book, And They Built A Crooked House, *which is 246 pages with appendices. In this account I have omitted the angst, the passion, the shear emotional trauma bared in the original book. Also left out are quotes from the depositions and trial, exhibits introduced in court including experts' reports, the bulk of the Judge's written Opinion, and my letters to the newspapers and community leaders. (As with the first book, in this synopsis I have changed the names of our developer, builder, architect and trial lawyer.) Those who wish to read the unabridged story, with all the documents included, may order* And They Built A Crooked House *directly from the publisher. Ordering information is in the last page of this book.*

Although what follows is a shortened version of the story, it is sufficient to show some of the inherent pitfalls in building or buying a new house. As will become evident from information presented in Section 2, every case is unique and every case is the same; the details may vary but the legal and financial effects are remarkably similar everywhere. So, too, are the emotional effects. Buying a seriously defective new house is a devastating experience no matter who you are, no matter what your profession. Though I am obviously critical of the people we did business with, perhaps the real culprit in ours and all other cases is a legal system that allows bad builders and developers to get away with — indeed, to profit by — their incompetence and/or dishonesty. If you think this is too strong a statement, read on. This book may help protect you from a similar disaster.

Headline

The following headline and lead paragraph appeared prominently in the Cleveland Plain Dealer on July 2, 1989.

Dream home turns into nightmare

...In July 1985, the Martins decided to take the plunge. They agreed to buy the land from the developer, Jake Cooper. The builder would be Murdock Construction Inc. and the architect James R. Nelson.

...None of those involved in building the house had bad reputations. But all would later be named as defendants in a lawsuit brought by the Martins...

If you own a home it is undoubtedly your biggest material asset. Imagine that your home suddenly lost half its market value, every dollar of equity disappeared, and you could not sell it for the value of your mortgage. A fire? An earthquake? Some other natural disaster?

For us the disaster was entirely manmade. After moving into a new $350,000 custom-built, architect-designed house, we discovered major defects, a result of both faulty design and construction. The developer — the man who arranged for construction and sold us the house — totally ignored our plight. The architect and builder, both men hired by the developer, refused to accept responsibility for the defects. Our construction contract, which we thought protected us in a major dispute, was simply ignored by all parties.

As a result my husband and I became plaintiffs in the largest residential construction case ever tried in Ohio, and one of the largest in the country. For three full years — the time we lived in the house — we suffered unremitting frustration and aggravation, not to mention enormous expense to fight our case. Yet what happened to us was entirely preventable. Our story may help you prevent a similar disaster.

Our saga began innocently enough, in the summer of 1985, when we decided to look for a larger house. Our family (three daughters, ages 2, 8 and 13) was outgrowing the old house. After 6 weeks of searching we found nothing suitable and affordable in the used-house market. Then we noticed a classified ad for a new 'spec' house being completed in an adjacent community. This house turned out to be smaller than we wanted, but we learned that a vacant 2-acre lot on the same street was available.

We Meet The Developer And His Architect

The man who placed the ad met us at the vacant lot, which he owned. For us, the lot was ideal: heavily wooded, very private, and on a cul-de-sac street. Most importantly, the street was in the same excellent school district as our existing home. This man, who I will call Jake Cooper, had bought three contiguous vacant lots; the lot next to the one we visited he had sold to his son, who was building a house, and the third lot over contained the spec house.

Mr. Cooper was not the actual builder, but proclaimed himself the 'developer' of houses on his land. To buy the vacant lot we would have to use Mr. Cooper's architect and builder, the same men erecting his son's house next door and the adjacent spec house. The price of the house would include his architect's fee and all financing until construction was completed, after a $30,000 down payment. We figured if the builder and architect were good enough for Mr. Cooper's son, they were good enough for us, and arranged to meet with Mr. Cooper's architect, James R. Nelson.

Mr. Nelson, was amiable and accommodating. He listened patiently to what we wanted (first floor master bedroom, four bedrooms upstairs, full basement), and over the next few weeks translated our wishes into a complete set of plans. It was the first time we had ever dealt with an architect, and remember feeling satisfied with his effort and drafting ability. We obviously had no idea at the time that he was incompetent to design our house or that, like the developer he worked for, he would lie once his mistakes were discovered.

The final plans called for a two-story, cedar-sided structure of 3800 square feet, plus a full, unfinished basement. Mr. Cooper's price came to $307,350 including the lot, close to what we had estimated. We did not bargain for a lower price. The reason we did not is, in retrospect, ironic. We felt that holding out for a lower price might give him some incentive to cut corners. We would rather pay his asking price and be assured of a well-built house.

We had still not met Mr. Cooper's builder, but weren't too concerned. The builder, Frank T. Murdock, was erecting Cooper Jr's home as well as the spec house, he was active in the area, and we had heard nothing bad about him (but then, we never asked). Also, Mr. Nelson, whom we trusted as a licensed professional, spoke highly of the builder. Again, we had not the slightest clue that these men were ignorant of how to design and build our house.

On several occasions, well before the contract signing, we asked Mr. Cooper what his responsibility and role would be.

"I am the developer," he said. "Mr. Murdock will build your house, but I am the developer, this is my project."

"Who do we call if there are any problems?"

"You call me. I am responsible."

Oh, how the lambs are deceived.

We Meet The Builder

We first met the builder in our lawyer's office the day of contract signing, November 8, 1985. A young man, Mr. Murdock had a rather breezy, confident air; he answered all our questions with a don't-worry-I-can-take-care-of-it attitude. Since we didn't know Mr. Murdock and had not hired him, we insisted that the architect, Mr. Nelson, make three inspections of the house during construction. Mr. Cooper, the developer, agreed and our contract lawyer wrote these inspections into the contract, which Mr. Cooper then signed. (Mr. Cooper had a separate construction contract with the builder.)

We felt positive about the deal. Many people were building

expensive homes in this Cleveland suburb, and our enterprise seemed almost risk-free. Mr. Cooper, an affluent, semi-retired jewelry salesman, was putting up most of the money; the architect and builder were working for him on the two adjacent houses; and we had a detailed contract. What could go wrong? Everything, as it turned out. We had unknowingly signed a contract with one unscrupulous businessman, and our house was about to be built by two other people who did not — quite literally — know how to do it.

Ground was broken in mid-November, 1985 and for the next eight months construction went smoothly, or so we thought. In February 1986, after one of his inspections, Mr. Nelson wrote us a letter on his firm's stationery, stating that everything was going well and that "Your home is one of our stronger designs."

The Developer Demands More Money

The contract originally called for a closing of May 15, 1986, but on May 17 the driveway wasn't finished. Also, Mr. Cooper had inexplicably not delivered the warranty deed to the bank on time, so a May 15 closing was not possible. For these reasons, and since the sale of our old house would not finalize for another few weeks, we asked for an extension of the closing to June 6. Mr. Cooper agreed in writing, without any dissent.

On June 5 Mr. Cooper dropped a bombshell. He walked into our lawyer's office and demanded an extra $1700 for "our delays." This was our first hint that written agreements and contracts meant nothing to Mr. Cooper.

Our lawyer called my husband at work to relay the demand. It was incredible. Mr. Cooper threatened to withhold the deed unless we agreed to pay more! After some haggling over the phone Mr. Cooper lowered his demand by half. He did not require a signed note, just a promise that we would pay him an extra $850 by the end of the year. His timing, reasoning and manner were perverse, irrational. He had no basis, legal or otherwise, for demanding extra money, but we had no choice. We had sold our old house and would soon have no place to live. So we agreed and he released the deed.

We moved in on June 17, 1986.

We Discover Sloping Floors — And More

Soon after moving in we noted problems with the house. The master bathroom shower leaked through to the basement ceiling tiles. The laundry room floor sloped. The kitchen and dining room floors sloped and walls in several rooms bowed out, apparent when we tried to hang pictures. (We appreciated none of these defects on our final inspection tour in May.)

We notified the builder, Mr. Murdock, and he promised to fix everything.   At this point we were not too concerned, and continued to spend money on our new home, adding landscaping, a wood deck, storm windows and other extras.   By December 1987 our total net investment in the house was $350,450. (Some of the additions, such as finishing the basement and a burglar alarm, were accomplished during construction.)

As the year progressed more defects became apparent, including: cracks in the basement floor and walls; water in the basement after a heavy rain; sloping floors in the foyer, family room and master bathroom; and an ill-fitting tub that shifted in its cradle when filled with water. The builder's repair attempts were never effective.   His workmen, when they did show up, seemed unable or unwilling to fix any of the major problems.

Several workmen came to look at the shower.   The tile man blamed the shower door. The shower door man blamed the tile work.   They replaced some tiles and adjusted the shower door, but the shower continued to leak.

On December 15, 1986 we wrote the builder and developer a polite but firm letter, listing all the defects and pleading with them to fix our house completely.

Mr. Cooper's response was to send a brief letter reminding us that we still owed him $850! He mentioned nothing about our letter or our construction problems. (Although his son lived next door and he visited there often, Mr. Cooper never once asked to see our home.) We responded with another detailed letter to both the developer and builder, pointing out their legal obligation to fix our house. Despite further letters from us and our lawyers, Mr. Cooper was never again heard from until he was sued, seven months later.

The Problems Continue

In January, 1987 Mr. Nelson came to investigate our complaints. Afterwards, he wrote us a detailed letter, stating that the house was structurally sound and that the sloping kitchen floor was an "optical illusion." He did acknowledge the sloping laundry room floor, and recommended adding latex material underneath the tile to level the floor. At no time did he even hint of any problem with his design.

The builder still couldn't get anything fixed properly. His workmen tried to level the laundry room floor by jacking it up from below with a vertical beam, but this only caused a large buckle in the dining room wall above. New joists were added to the basement ceiling but the floors above still sloped. Crooked door frames that held our pocket doors were replaced; the new frames were even more crooked! The more problems we encountered, first with the house, then with the builder's feeble attempts to fix things, the more defensive he became.

We called our contract lawyer and on February 12, 1987 he wrote a letter to the builder and developer, threatening legal action if the house wasn't soon fixed. Our fury was rising. We began a detailed log of all the delays and problems with the builder's workmen. Now anticipating a lawsuit, we sent out a third letter to all three men, and included our "Log of Daily Frustrations."

About this time, in response to months of complaining, the leaky shower was finally fixed. The rubber liner underneath the tile had a hole in it! When asked why this problem wasn't discovered months earlier, the plumber responded: "We check the simplest things first."

The Final Straw

In late February Mr. Murdock came to the house with his head carpenter, and now appeared willing to fix all the other defects. This change in his attitude was more a response to our contract lawyer's threatening letter than to our own correspondence. Over the next few days Murdock's workmen ripped out walls, lifted flooring, and removed moldings in various parts of the house. We were encouraged. Nothing had yet been repaired during all this activity, but the builder at least seemed motivated.

Then on March 2 the builder sent a "junior carpenter" to fix the sloping mudroom floor. The method? Irregular pieces of particle board that left a gaping hole through to the basement. The result was appallingly sloppy — and the floor still sloped!

At that point we became convinced the builder didn't know what he was doing and oh, were we right! We called and asked him to desist from further repair attempts until we obtained an independent investigation of our house. His response to what was clearly a botched construction job:

"I can only do what my architect tells me."

Not only did Murdock not understand the construction defects, he also did not accept responsibility. His response was a taste of things to come.

The Experts Descend

On the advice of our contract lawyer we hired an attorney experienced in trial work, a litigator, someone I'll call Tom Baxter. Hiring a litigator is like being operated on by a surgeon; both specialists control your destiny, except that the litigator's control lasts as long as the lawsuit exists. You are totally at his mercy and — except for firing him — can do nothing on your own about the lawsuit.

The first thing Mr. Baxter did was to contact experts for a detailed investigation. Within a month this group included a consulting architect, a structural engineer, a soils analyst, and a builder. Initial cost for just these experts was over $5000. Coupled with our lawyer's fee of $145 per hour, we began spending an average of *$1000/week* to pursue our case.

By early May we received the reports. The house was defective throughout, both by design (inadequate support beams; structural tolerances below the standard of locally-accepted building codes) and construction (substandard rough-in carpentry; sloppy and substandard craftsmanship). Both the architect's understanding and the builder's repair attempts were way off the mark. To fix the house properly would cost almost $100,000 and we would have to move out for at least three months!

We were devastated, but felt confident that these men would not want a lawsuit, especially since the evidence for defective design and construction was so blatant. We could not have been more wrong.

From the time we first viewed the lot until the day of contract signing, the developer Mr. Cooper had always made it clear that he was responsible for our house, and that the builder and architect were his agents. We had not even met Mr. Murdock, the builder, before the day of contract signing, and we had no contract with either him or the architect. It was Mr. Cooper who placed the classified ad about the property, hired the architect and builder, sold us the house, and pocketed the profit (we found out later his profit on the deal was over $50,000). Yet we would have to spend tens of thousands of dollars to get to trial and prove the developer's responsibility. And even then we would lose everything.

With disastrous consequences for us, our contract lawyer had failed to assign specific responsibility in the event of major construction mistakes. He had inserted an ambiguous clause whereby the developer's separate construction agreement with the builder was "assigned" to us. This clause was to protect us in the event Mr. Cooper died or skipped town during construction, but instead Mr. Cooper used it to claim "no responsibility" for the problems with our house. His claim was mind-boggling since, in another part of the contract, Mr. Cooper specifically guaranteed "first class, workmanlike construction."

Our contract also did not make either the builder or developer responsible for the architect, a person we had not hired. Although architects are independent professionals, our architect did not have malpractice insurance — he was totally bare. If any of the problems were due to his faulty design, then we could be in the situation of having to sue a man we had not hired or paid, and who was neither wealthy nor insured. We had never considered (or been told about) this legal 'black hole.'

The builder did carry builder's insurance, but his insurance company saw the architect's involvement as a way to avoid paying for any structural repairs.

We File a Lawsuit

Here's what happened. After receiving our experts' reports in May, 1987, the builder's insurance company claimed the problems were 90% the architect's mistakes, and refused to repair the house. The architect — when confronted with all the evidence — acknowledged that his design included two undersized steel beams. He agreed to strengthen these beams, but not correct any other defects. Such strengthening would correct only a fraction of the total defects, and could not be accomplished without a commitment to fix the rest of the house, which the builder's insurer refused to consider. In fact the builder's insurer made *no* offer to fix anything, not even the cosmetic defects obviously the builder's responsibility.

And Mr. Cooper? He refused to respond. Despite several attorney letters and the obvious threat of a lawsuit, Mr. Cooper remained silent throughout the spring and summer. As a result of this impasse, on July 22, 1987 we filed one of Ohio's largest residential construction lawsuits.

The suit asked for recision of the contract: a demand that Mr. Cooper buy back the house at its full market value, plus pay all our expenses. The suit clearly spelled out Mr. Cooper's breach of the written contract, wherein he guaranteed us a home built in a "first class workmanlike manner." The suit also demanded, of all three defendants, monetary damages for our emotional suffering and aggravation.

Over and over again we asked ourselves: 'How can it be that we hired a lawyer in order to avoid problems, and now have this legal nightmare?' Yet our litigator refused to blame the contract lawyer. "A contract is only as good as the people behind it. You just had a bad result," he kept telling us. He did not consider this "bad result" sufficient grounds to sue the contract lawyer.

Fortunately we were able to live in the house, but that did not ease the pain of knowing what we had bought. In July 1987 we had the house formally appraised. Without defects it was valued at $410,000 (reflecting the rapid appreciation of homes in our area). With the defects: $251,000, a figure arrived at simply by subtracting the total cost to restore and resell the home. But who would buy such a wreck?

In November 1987 we put the house on the market through a real estate agent. Because of the defects the house could only be shown to people in the construction business. Furthermore, our experts' reports had to be disclosed or *we* could be sued. The highest offer received was $202,000, from a local builder. This amount was not enough to cover our mortgage (after real estate commission) and meant we could not move if we wanted to. We had lost every dollar of equity.

Meanwhile the lawsuit was like a big yawn. Mr. Cooper did respond to the suit, but only to deny *any* responsibility. The other two defendants denied the extent of our claim and admitted only to relatively minor defects. One would think the insurance company's lawyer would realize the magnitude of the situation and offer to settle. Not so. Instead, he did nothing to investigate our complaints and denied his client's responsibility for anything more than cosmetic defects; he assigned all structural problems to the architect.

We continued to run up legal and expert fees, as our lawyer met with their lawyers, our experts met with their experts, and all the lawyers met with the Judge. Between August 1987 and February 1988 there were five pre-trial hearings, none of which accomplished anything.

In late 1987 our lawyer received two strange letters from the builder's insurance company lawyer. The first letter (October 1987) proposed that the insurer fix the undisputed items (perhaps 20% of the estimated defects) and then "proceed with further litigation on the disputed items." This offer was turned down flat. The last thing we wanted was to have the house partially fixed and continue the litigation.

The second letter (December 1987) was even more provocative. The builder's lawyer wrote: "...it is unbelievable that your clients have done nothing since March 9, 1987 to mitigate the damages claimed against [the builder]...especially when all of the alleged construction defects could have been remedied within a week."

In retrospect it seems these letters were ploys to make it seem they wanted to settle, but really to guarantee there would be a trial. A trial builds up big legal fees. For the lawyer paid by an insurance company, of course, that's a windfall. For us, the plaintiffs, paying out of pocket, it is a disaster. We were becoming enmeshed in a totally no-win situation, one destined to deplete our savings and enrich all the lawyers. We felt, at the time, that we had no choice but to pursue this quest for justice. Our lawyer never guaranteed a victory, but he also never appraised us of our no-win position.

The Case Drags On

The Judge came to visit the house in January 1988 and (according to our attorney) seemed appalled by what he saw. Still, the case would rest on expert opinion. Seeing the damage didn't solve the issue of responsibility.

Our legal and expert fees continued to climb. The developer and architect were deposed in early 1988, along with their two experts, one hired by the architect, the other by the builder's insurer. Mr. Cooper stated, in his deposition, that he had "no responsibility" for our house, and cited the ambiguous paragraph in our contract.

The architect's deposition revealed him to be well meaning but inept (his blatant lying came later). As for the two 'experts,' the one hired by the builder's insurer never seriously investigated the house. He did not submit a written report, at least none seen by us. His initial 'impression' that the floors did not slope was later demolished by a detailed engineering survey of the house.

The other expert, hired by the architect, also did not investigate the house. His opinions were based on some information about grades of lumber provided by the architect, and turned out to be unrelated to the house's structural problems. Subsequently neither of these experts was called to testify at trial.

Because of some concern about weakness of our first structural engineer in a court fight, in January 1988 our lawyer called in a more experienced structural engineer to examine the house. This second engineer surmised that the floors were built sloping, which put much of the blame on the builder. "No one used a level when they built this house," he said.

In February 1988 Mr. Cooper's lawyer called in a new expert, an engineer who examined the floors for sloping. Using a vertical rod and surveying telescope, he went from room to room to check for sloping floors. (He was the only defense expert who systematically surveyed the house and filed a written report). His survey found the degree of sloping greater than even we had determined, in some areas as much as 1 to 2 inches in 20 feet!

With evidence in hand from our second structural engineer and Mr. Cooper's engineer, our attorney arranged for experts from both sides to meet. At this meeting, held in our attorney's law offices on February 18, 1988 the experts reached a consensus: our house *was* designed and built defectively. The two major structural defects are schematically diagramed on the next page.

Schematic of Major Structural Defects

Center columns (CC) throughout the basement are not level with outside basement walls (OW), causing sloping of horizontal steel beams (B) toward the center. As a result, both the first and second floors slope toward the center of the house. This defect was attributed to the builder.

Distance between outside basement walls and center columns is too long for the size of beams (B) used in several areas. As a result, these beams are undersized and sag in the middle, causing more sloping of the floors above. This defect was attributed to the architect.

These defects do not affect the outside frame walls (F), which remain straight.

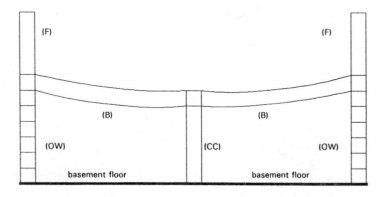

At the February 18 meeting the experts agreed that proper repair would require adding structural supports throughout the house, plus "jacking up the house and leveling all the floors." A dollar cost was not discussed, nor was the question of responsibility, by now the central legal issue in the case. Still, despite agreement on the defects there was *no* offer to fix the house.

Instead, on April 13 and 14, 1988 we were deposed by the three defense attorneys. The builder's insurance lawyer asked most of the questions. It seemed to us that he was using our depositions to learn about the case, and that his two previous letters reflected either unwarranted arrogance or simple ignorance of the facts (or both). For over nine hours he painstakingly went through almost every letter and document, asking us to confirm the dates, our signatures, and other self-evident information.

Along the way he probed to determine what kind of people we are. Have we ever sued anyone before? No. Did we have any problems with Mr. Cooper or the builder before we moved in? None. Have we taken any tax deductions because of our defective house? No. Who have we told about our house? Only our closest friends. Why did we put the house on the market? To sell it and get on with our lives. Why didn't we sell it? Because we couldn't afford to buy another house with the offers received. Did we know any of the experts before they were called in? No. Why are we suing for recision instead of full repairs? Because we have three children and don't want to move twice.

In truth, our claim was so honest, straightforward and provable that the defendants' lawyers seemed embarrassed. They came into the depositions thinking we must be ogres. We believe they left feeling somewhat ashamed of their clients. Our lawyer said he had never before seen such believable and unassailable testimony. He wished the Judge could have been there.

We did not fool ourselves for one second into thinking we had won our case. There was still no offer to fix the house and we knew there would be a trial. By blaming someone else, each defendant obviously felt he could come out ahead in court. Certainly the defense lawyers stood to make a bundle by going to court. (Our lawyer eventually put a ceiling on his fees, so that he would make nothing extra by going to trial.)

We also knew we could win legally and still lose big. How? By a judgment that omitted all our legal and experts' expenses ($55,000 by the time of trial). Or by an order to fix the house, making us move twice and go through the aggravation of reconstruction. Or by a judgment against Mr. Cooper and/or the architect that led to a declaration of bankruptcy. Or by a decision that resulted in endless appeals and more litigation.

Trial vs. Settlement

Our first trial was scheduled for May 16, 1988. A few days earlier, our builder expert was deposed. After his deposition Tom came over to the house to tell us the bad news. The builder's deposition was a disaster. Tom had not properly prepared the builder, and apparently there was much confusion when his itemized figures to repair the house didn't add up to his original estimate. We were devastated, and disappointed in our attorney. He would go to trial but now didn't feel comfortable. For our part, we wanted nothing more than to get this nightmare over with. It was almost two years since we had we moved in, 18 months after our first letter to the developer and builder, and 10 months after the suit was filed.

We went to the courthouse on May 16, as scheduled. Right away, all the lawyers huddled. After about an hour Tom came out and said the builder's insurer agreed to fix the house! If we insisted on a trial we might win (even with our expert's shaky testimony), but with appeals the case could drag on for years. He recommended we strongly consider the offer. We agreed.

Five hours later, after non-stop negotiations, the lawyers reached a verbal 'settlement'. It would have to be put in writing by our attorney and then signed by all parties, a process that would take about two weeks.

Basically the defendants, in partnership with the builder's insurer, agreed to pay an independent contractor to fix the entire house, pay all move-out expenses and most of our expert fees (except for the first structural engineer). They would not pay for our legal fees. (In Ohio, legal fees are not recoverable unless you win damages at trial, something our lawyer considered unlikely.)

As unfair as such a settlement would be (we had bought a new house and now stood to lose tens of thousands just to get those responsible to fix it), our lawyer thought it preferable to going to trial. He was right of course, but then all we had at that point were promises from dishonest men. My husband and I did not believe their verbal offer was sincere; we simply had no reason to trust them. Our lawyer was also concerned, since the defendants had never before shown any interest in properly fixing the house.

To protect us against a phony offer, Tom drafted a Settlement Agreement that would allow us to resume the original recision suit if there was a "material breach of the Agreement," i.e., if the defendants signed it and did nothing, or made only desultory repairs. Without such a clause, he said, we could be substituting one piece of paper for another, and in the process lose our right to sue for recision. On the other hand, if they fixed the house properly, we would drop the lawsuit "without prejudice."

On May 26 the Settlement Agreement was mailed out. All the lawyers met again on June 3. The defendants refused to accept the Agreement! Their attorneys offered no explanation. There was no stated objection to any specific part of the Agreement; instead, they simply refused it. The trial was once again rescheduled, for October 11, 1988.

We began to despair of the legal system. Five pretrial hearings, a phony offer on the day of trial, seemingly endless delay and expenses. How can this happen? How is it that people obviously responsible for a home's defects can be allowed to jerk around the innocent, wronged homeowners? How can they be allowed to spend many thousands on legal fees instead of spending it to fix our house? We had (and have) no answers to these questions. It is the 'legal system' and there's nothing plaintiffs can do about it. We just prayed for the ordeal to end.

(By the summer of 1988 this legal cancer had invaded every part of our existence, affecting our relations with each other, and with our children, friends and relatives. At times the emotional strain was so incredible that, in hindsight, we feel fortunate to have kept our health and our sanity. We worked hard to continue living normally; these men destroyed our home but we wouldn't let them destroy our lives.)

Tom took advantage of the long delay to bring in another contractor for a more detailed repair estimate. To strengthen the case our lawyer wanted a detailed, line-item estimate that would be more defensible in court.

After six visits to the house during July and August, 1988, the new contractor arrived at a figure close to the first repair estimate: $92,000. His estimate included jacking up the house, adding new structural supports, leveling the floors, and waterproofing the basement, plus repairing all the interior damage that might result form this work.

Perhaps realizing his mistake in preparing for the first trial, Tom made some arrangements to limit his fees. For another $14,000, payable before the trial, everything else would be on contingency. Any money we received to fix the house or to sell it would be ours totally. His firm would receive 40% of any money we received for damages. Did he really expect to win damages against these men? We hoped so, and readily signed the contingency agreement. This arrangement at least fixed our legal and experts' expenses at around $55,000 to $60,000, no matter how long the trial took (appeals were not covered, however).

Trial

The trial began on October 11, 1988 and lasted five days, but spanned two weeks (there was a week's hiatus when the Judge had to go out of town for another case). In those five days we proved our case. In addition to our own testimony and mountains of written documents (including our letters and numerous photographs and drawings) we called four witnesses — the consultant architect, structural engineer, consultant builder to present his estimate, and the real estate agent who tried to sell the house in November, 1987. They all gave effective testimony.

Tom tried to get testimony about the formal appraisal of our house entered into the record, but it was not allowed. The market value of the house was not considered legally relevant. The Judge also disallowed any testimony about legal fees, since without a provable case of fraud they were not recoverable.

The defense lawyers tried to discredit the testimony of our witnesses, but that was difficult in light of the facts. In the end the defense presented only one expert, the developer's engineer who had surveyed for sloping floors, and he mainly corroborated the defects. His testimony was used to minimize the amount of necessary repairs. For example, he did not think the floors would need as much attention to leveling after the jacking-up process as did our engineer.

When questioned about the problems on cross examination, Mr. Cooper's engineer said they were "not insurmountable." He also admitted that he would "not guarantee" the results of reconstruction.

The defendants did not have much to say for themselves. Nelson the architect admitted design errors and the builder admitted to construction mistakes (finally!). Cooper the developer said he had never responded to us because "other people" were taking care of the problems. He also denied threatening to withhold the deed if we didn't agree to pay more money (a lie), but did not explain why he demanded more money in the first place.

Cooper also testified that he called the builder every time he received one of our letters (another lie), and that he was "concerned" about our problems. Murdock testified that the developer called him only once. Their conflicting testimony did not seem to matter to the court. In fact nothing outside the demonstrable defects seemed legally relevant. (Immediately after his testimony Cooper asked for permission to fly to Italy for a "buying trip." It was inconceivable to us that someone being sued would fly out of the country in the middle of his trial. But Cooper didn't seem in the least concerned. Permission was granted and he flew to Italy after the second day of his trial).

Despite the mountain of evidence we presented, both to prove the house's defects and the defendants' culpability and bad faith, the law (or the Judge's interpretation of it) could not make us "whole," that is, restore our losses. Ohio laws — as is true in every other state I have heard or read about — do not, apparently, provide for restoring one's home to its proper value, reimbursing expenses, or compensating the victimized homeowner for lost time and aggravation. As a result, practically every attempt to introduce testimony about costs beyond simple repair of our house was objected to by the defendants' lawyers and sustained by the Judge.

On the last day of trial each defense lawyer gave his summary statement; each agreed to some defects in the house, but tried to minimize his client's role. The developer's lawyer laid the problems on the architect and builder. If his client was ordered to buy the house back it should be for no more than $307,350 (the basic contract price) since, he argued, "recision is supposed to return the parties to their state before the contract."

The architect's attorney said his client was only responsible for about $8,000, what it would cost to repair the design errors; however, he had offered no testimony on this point during the trial. The builder's insurance company lawyer said that our repair estimate was absurdly high. Although none of the three defense attorneys had offered *any* testimony in court about the cost of repairs, the builder's attorney blithely started subtracting items *he* thought were unnecessary, and in this manner ended up at "$25,000." (If that's all it cost, one wonders why the defendants never followed through on their offer to fix the house.)

Tom argued for one of two judgments: either the full amount for us to make the repairs (and move out during the process), or recision at the house's fair market price. Since the market value of the house wasn't allowed into testimony, our attorney instead asked for interest on the total purchase price of $350,000; interest on this amount approximated the appreciation our home should have realized from June 1986. For either decision our lawyer also argued that we were entitled to a monetary award to cover our experts' fees and an additional large award for the emotional suffering caused by the defendants' breach of contract.

The Judge listened patiently to all the arguments, then announced that his decision would take "at least a week."

Decision

The trial ended October 24. For the next five weeks we heard nothing. Then, on December 1 our lawyer called with the news. We won and we lost.

IN THE COURT OF COMMON PLEAS (Cuyahoga County)
CASE NO. 133316
<u>**FINDING OF THE COURT**</u>
<u>**RESCISSION**</u>

"The evidence will show that the following list of problems must be corrected in order to place [our home] in the first quality condition required by the contract. The problems which must be corrected cannot possibly be characterized as anything other than material breaches. They are:

"To jack all rooms
To jack basement
To dig 2 footers for basement columns
To install footers around basement stairs
To install unsightly newell post in foyer or,
    alternatively, to double header
To rip floors in second floor to double joists, or
    alternatively, rip off walls to install plywood bracing
To remove and refloor laundry room
To pull out and build properly a significant portion of
    the master bath
To pull out and reinstall dining room walls
To patch, sand, tape, spackle virtually every room in
    the house resulting from jacking operation
To repaint all of the rooms
To apply leveling compound on floors that were not
    leveled by jacking

"This list is incomplete. The record is replete from numerous experts concerning the various problems that could be sustained to try to restore this house to a "first class, quality structure."

"One should understand that even these experts, with all the remedies they discuss, "could not guarantee" a solution to the problem.

"If the best of all the remedies were completed, the plaintiff still, if they were to attempt to sell the house, would be buying (or selling) a lawsuit from the new purchasers.

"The time and cost to repair is enormous in light of the price paid and the guarantees made.

"The court orders rescission [legal term for buy-back] in the amount of $307,350 for the purchase price plus $42,218 for improvements for a total of $349,568."

* * *

In another section of the Judge's 12-page decision, he ordered the builder to pay $20,172, and the architect $18,718, directly to the developer for repairs. The total of $38,890 was far less than our experts had estimated, but it didn't matter to us since fixing the house was no longer our option. According to the Judge, if we made repairs and then tried to sell the house we would be incurring another lawsuit.

One reason the total awarded the developer was lower than our experts' estimates was that the Judge did not grant money to waterproof the basement; instead he stipulated that the "exterior of the basement walls and basement wall must be warranted by [the builder] to [the developer]." Another reason, presumably, is that the developer heads his own construction company, and could get the repairs done much cheaper than we would have to pay.

In his decision the Judge did not explain the discrepancy between our actual cost of $350,450 for the house and his recision price of $349,568. The only additional item we were awarded was moving expenses (to be collected from the builder and architect).

The Judge also gave no reason for not granting us any of our experts' fees, even though he extensively used reports of these same experts to write his opinion. Nor was there any statement about entitlement to interest, appreciation, or an award for emotional damages. The way these men responded to our complaint and the way they treated us — the architect inspecting our house during construction and missing all the defects; the developer ignoring all letters from us and from our attorneys; the architect telling us in writing that obviously sloping floors were an optical illusion; the failure of all three defendants to properly investigate our complaints; reneging on an offer to fix the house in May 1988, causing trial postponement; and their lack of any offer at any time to fix our house properly — was all legally irrelevant.

In summary, despite the fact that every aspect of our house as anything other than shelter had been destroyed, despite the fact that *we* had to pay thousands to prove what *they* had done to our home, and despite the fact that the developer had guaranteed us a first class home and then refused to respond until sued — despite all this, the Judge saw our case as only one of a 'breached contract.' As victims of a breached contract, he obviously felt we could not recover *anything* beyond what we spent on the defective house.

Motion for Amendment

Obviously this was an unfair decision. Not only were we out a huge amount of money despite *winning* our case, but the developer stood to make a second profit. He could fix the house and then sell it for well over $350,000. The estimated market value as of March 1989, if the house had been properly built, was between 450 and 475 thousand dollars. Considering the house's history he might not get that much, but any sale over $350,000 would represent a profit. Our loss would literally be his gain.

Had the government appropriated our property to build a highway, we would have been paid the appraised value of the house. Had our home burned to the ground the insurance company would have paid for its replacement at current market value. But this is not what happened. What happened was not an act of nature or a result of government policy. What happened was that incompetent and uncaring men, men who had made specific guarantees in writing, had built our home defectively and thereby destroyed its market value and, in addition, caused us to incur enormous added costs. For *this* act, for which responsibility was clear and direct, the law (or the Judge interpreting the law) did not recognize our home's replacement value or any of the costs we incurred to prove our case. Whatever the reasoning, the decision made no sense to us.

Actually, the Judge's decision appeared counter to the philosophy behind Ohio real estate law.* This was our attorney's

----

* "The philosophy of the law is to place the aggrieved party in the same economic position he would have been in but for the breach of contract. If the party would have made profits off the contract, the profits are properly included. He should be compensated for any losses sustained. Some common compensatory damages seen in real estate actions are awards of the real estate commission, interest rate differences, points, additional moving costs, and additional rental costs." (Ohio Real Estate Law, 3rd edition, CK Irvin and JD Irvin, Gorsuch Scarisbrick Publishers, Scottsdale, AZ, 1985.)

assessment, and on December 9 Tom filed a Motion for Amendment of the decision. This Motion is not an appeal but only a request, in the form of a legal brief, for the Judge to reconsider certain aspects of the decision. Citing legal precedents in other cases, our lawyer asked the Judge to grant us 2 years' interest on the $349,568, plus our experts' fees and closing costs.

After receiving a counter brief from the Developer's attorney, and a rebuttle from our lawyer, on January 20, 1989 the Judge issued a one word response to our Motion: "Overruled."

*   *   *

Imagine that you have just discovered a major defect in your house and that, in consequence of your complaint, you are ordered by the court to sell your home for $100,000 less than it is worth. Imagine that the defect was manmade and no fault of your own. Add to this scenario $55,000 for expenses plus three years of unremitting aggravation. Finally, imagine there is nothing you can do about it without losing more money and incurring more aggravation. Now you have some idea of what happened to us.

A contractor could infer the following message from the outcome of our case: If he builds a defective home he can ignore the homeowners totally until a lawsuit is filed. He can ignore and deny everything as long as he shows up at trial. If he loses, the worst that can happen is that he'll have to buy the house back, but then only at the original price. He will not have to pay for any appreciation, or for the homeowners' legal or experts' fees. The longer he can delay the trial the more he'll gain as the property appreciates. In essence, selling a defective new home is a 'no-risk' situation; as long as property values appreciate, the contractor can be as incompetent and uncaring as he wishes and he will still come out ahead. If justice is delayed long enough he can conceivably get the property back at just what the land is worth!

Based on what happened to us, the developer of defective homes in Ohio cannot lose. Only the homeowner can lose. We were out over $55,000 in expenses, at least $100,000 in lost appreciation, and another $6000 in closing costs.

(Every case is unique and one could argue that a judge acting fairly would have compensated us fairly; after all, we did prove both the defects and material breach of contract. True, but the result epitomizes a theme of this book, which is prevention. You don't ever want to trust your plight to the mercy of a judge or jury or arbitrator. They may view evidence one way on Monday and another on Thursday. One judge may allow unlimited delays while another judge moves your case swiftly along. Or one judge may keep valid testimony from being heard while another judge admits all arguments. And so on. The legal process is highly arbitrary, and heavily stacked against people seeking redress in a civil matter. In breach of contract cases, where the legal outcome is meaningless unless you recoup your monetary losses, the plaintiff can lose in many more ways than he can win.)

Despite our enormous losses and the peculiar logic exhibited by the Judge in our case, we decided not to appeal. In essence the Judge had ordered us to return something that only goes *up* in value (real estate in a prime location) in exchange for something that only goes *down* in value (a fixed sum of money). For this reason appeal was a no-win situation. Any further delay by appealing would mean just a greater loss when the time came to buy another house, plus the legal expense of appealing. Even if a higher court granted us interest on the $349,568, the dollar amount would not equal the rapid appreciation of homes in our area. We had no rational choice but to stem our losses and move out. We had built our dream home and, through no fault of our own, lost a fortune.

We Move

After all our petitions were exhausted in January 1989, we began to look for another home. We were shocked to see how much used houses had gone up since 1985. The good schools had attracted an influx of people and as a result old houses had jumped between 30% and 60% in four years! It was disheartening to see homes smaller than ours, on a less desirable lot, going for over $500,000.

We had no choice but to double our mortgage payments or accept a lesser home. Having lost a fortune we opted for the

latter. In late February we bought a 20-year-old split level house
for $340,000. In 1985, when we contracted for our custom-built
disaster, this split level would have sold in the mid-$200,000
range.

We moved into our new home June 22, 1989. Although a nice
house, in size and amenities it doesn't compare with what we had
built. For almost the same price we ended up with a far smaller
lot and garage, and without a first floor master bedroom, finished
basement, or deck. Still, we have no complaints about this house
except the $160,000 'extra' we spent getting here.

Lies and Deception

> Half the truth is often a great lie.
> — Benjamin Franklin, Poor Richard's Almanack, 1758

Throughout the spring of 1989 there was no escaping the awful
feeling of injustice. We were, in effect, ordered to move out of
our new home at a $160,000 loss. Meanwhile, Cooper was
preparing to take another profit on the dwelling. He had gained
the upper hand by choosing to *not* respond, had in fact totally
ignored us and our contract with a claim of "no responsibility."
We could not (and still cannot) fathom how the law can penalize
buyers of a defective home and, at the same time, reward a
developer like Jake Cooper.

As you have seen, and as will again become apparent, the law
is virtually toothless against dishonest developers like Jake
Cooper. The decision had now put him in position to sell the
house, without proper repairs, to some unsuspecting family at
another profit. Would he dare? Yes, he would. Since
inspections that lead to an occupancy permit ignore structural
defects, he could also get away with it. Unless the authorities
knew what had happened to us, Cooper *could* profit from selling
a defective home twice.

Why did we care? Our losses were final, the case was over,
nothing we said or did could reimburse us even partly. But
reimbursement was no longer the point. We felt obligated to do
something for the rights of homeowners, especially whoever might
end up with our old house. The law may not be able to reach

men like Cooper, but perhaps something else could: publicity.

On June 23, 1989 I sent a letter to the mayor and council members of the community, telling them what happened, why we had moved, and asking that they not let this sorry episode repeat itself. Also, to clarify any misunderstanding about our reasons for moving I sent a copy to friends living on the street.

My letter alone should have sufficed to ensure that Cooper properly repaired the house, but I realized other people needed to also know. After all, the community might claim it had no responsibility to inspect a used home, or that the legal judgment superseded any local responsibility for the house.

I also sent a copy of the letter and the Judge's written opinion to the Cleveland Plain Dealer and two suburban papers. The reaction was quicker than expected, almost immediate. Shortly after we moved out we were phoned by a widely-read columnist for the Plain Dealer, and also by reporters for the suburban weeklies. The PD's story is the one quoted at the beginning of this section. The column ends:

For the three years the Martins lived in their new home, not a day went by that they weren't reminded of what a disaster it was. Worse yet, they took a financial bath in their legal victory...The Martins won, all right, but they're at least $155,000 poorer for their victory.

...They've also written a book about their dream-house experience...They can call it "Nightmare on [- - - -] Lane."

This column, plus a suburban newspaper story that appeared on July 6 ("Couple's dream house turns to horror story," Chagrin Valley Times), created intense publicity for awhile. In response, Cooper and Nelson (but not Murdock) held a news conference at our old house. Their comments were published in two long articles in the suburban weeklies (apparently no one from the Plain Dealer, Cleveland's daily newspaper, attended their conference).

At first we were surprised that Cooper would blab about the case, since he was proven in court to have breached his contract with us. But we were even more surprised that he would appear publicly with Nelson, the architect who was proven to have designed our house defectively.

It turns out Cooper was using Nelson to help make the repairs! As we read their comments, it became clearer just what type of people we had been up against. These men were egregious liars. The following quotes and comments from Architect Nelson appeared in news articles from the Chagrin Valley Times or the Chagrin Herald Sun, July 13, 1989.

> **"When I went over the plans with Mrs. Martin, she wanted a support column in the basement moved to open the area. It's a common request, but in removing the column, I failed to recalculate the loads (on the beam)."**

Not only was this statement a lie, but Nelson had never used this excuse before, in any letter, in deposition, or in court. Now he was blaming *me* for *his* design inadequacy.* Nelson also:

> **said he offered to fix [his design] problem, which he estimated would have cost $3000 to $5000, but the Martins chose to take legal action.**

Nelson's design defects were much more major than he was ever willing to fix. The Judge assessed them at over $18,000, a fact Mr. Nelson did not mention at his news conference.

Nelson did get one thing right, however:

> **"...the sloping floors, which were noticeable, were caused by flexed beams and basement columns set too low in the foundation, a construction error."**

----

* These excerpts typify the kind of revisionist history and distortions of fact that homeowner victims commonly face when a case goes public. In Section 2 you will find similar excuses given by builders in other areas of the country, to explain away defective construction and unhappy homeowners.

So Nelson blamed me for his design mistakes and lay the other structural problems on Murdock. Then, for the reporters, he tried to make it look like we wouldn't let him fix what was wrong with the house. How can you win against an architect who is not only incompetent, but who lies about his mistakes? You cannot.

And what did Jake Cooper claim? The following quotes are from the same July 13, 1989 articles that appeared in the Chagrin Valley Times and the Chagrin Herald Sun.

> **"I never heard from [the Martins]. They drew up the contract with me and passed all responsibility on to the builder and architect...And I responded to the builder when he gave me copies of their letters to him."**

Despite having received a total of *nine* letters from us and our lawyers Cooper claimed he *never* heard from us. And the "builder...gave me copies of their letters"? *ALL THE LETTERS WERE SENT DIRECTLY TO HIM!*

Cooper also claimed that:

> **"Everybody wanted to do the right thing. But [the Martins] were encouraged by somebody that they could get $2 million, so they didn't let the builder complete the repairs to the house...That's why they brought all their experts in."**

This comment, perhaps more than any other, shows the baseless character of the man we had done business with. But there were more lies from his twisted psyche.

> **Mr. Cooper said he did offer to settle out of court, contrary to the Martins' claim, and [Mr. Cooper] also claimed [the Martins] are the ones who reneged on an out-of-court settlement.**

And quoting Cooper directly:

> **"The whole thing got blown out of proportion. I was not unhappy with the house. That's why I didn't appeal the**

case."

> "I'll be lucky to get $375,000 for [the house]. You just
> don't get $400,000 on this block...I wish they would have
> stayed and let [the builder] fix their house."

Cooper was "not unhappy with the house" because he knew he
had been handed a windfall by the court: the house and lot at
1985 prices (in a rising market) *and* money to make the repairs.

In the aggregate, Cooper's and Nelson's comments showed that
we didn't have a chance in hell of getting our house fixed properly
during the litigation. Even *after* the trial and our experts'
testimony and the Judge's written opinion, neither Cooper nor
Nelson admitted to the defects or displayed any understanding of
why we went to trial. Nor, of course, did they have the slightest
remorse for what they had done to us.

According to our attorney, Cooper's lies and blatant distortion
of our motives were not sufficient grounds to sue for slander.
Still, I felt the need to set the record straight and countered with
a letter to the editor pointing out Cooper's lies (published in the
Chagrin Valley Times on August 17, 1989). Tom also sent a
strong letter to Cooper's attorney, serving notice that his client
should stop distorting the case or face a possible lawsuit.

The lies did not end there. Cooper proceeded to deceive
prospective home buyers. On August 3, 1989 he put the house up
for sale, advertising in the classifieds:

> **BY OWNER. VERY SPECIAL . . . 5 bedroom**
> **Contemporary. 2 Acre fully wooded lot on quiet**
> **cul-de-sac street . . . Ready now for occupancy.**
> **Low 400s.**

This ad appeared well *after* Cooper publicly stated "you just
don't get $400,000 on this street." Also, it is noteworthy that
three different experts estimated it would take at least three
months to fix our house properly. We moved out June 22 and
Cooper's ad appeared less than six weeks later.

Cooper did not sell the house 'by owner' so he signed up with
a large real estate company. Perhaps to explain how the house

came to be vacant, he told people that we had moved out of town and so he bought the house back, as if he had done us a favor. Worse, he wrote a deceitful open letter to explain his position with the house, and copies were distributed by the real estate agent to people who came to look at the house. Calling us by name, this letter stated that we had a "personality conflict" with the builder and became unhappy with the house. The letter made no mention of the lawsuit, the trial, the structural defects, the judgment or his breach of contract. Cooper's letter was shown to prospective buyers throughout the summer and early fall of 1989.

Our lawyer agreed that Cooper's outrageous and dishonest letter should not go unchallenged. On September 29, 1989 he sent a strongly worded letter to the president of the realty company, with a copy to the individual agents involved in marketing the house. Our lawyer's letter said, in effect, 'Mr. Cooper is lying and he better stop or you, the real estate company, could be sued.'

While all this was going on Cooper found a buyer, a couple with two kids moving from Florida to Cleveland. They were shown Cooper's deceptive letter. Cooper met with them. He led them to believe that he had bought the house back from us because we were "moving out of town." (In a metropolitan area of 456 square miles with a population of 1.5 million, we moved a distance of less than two miles, to an adjacent suburb within the same school district.)

Cooper didn't mention the lawsuit, the trial, the experts' reports, the newspaper publicity. He told them that only one area of the house was defective (the area under the mudroom floor, about 10% of what we proved in court), and that it had been fixed with some new posts. This out-of-town couple bid $368,000 for the house and it was accepted.

Then they found out we were still in town and called us. We told them the simple truth. The house had major defects. There was a lawsuit. A trial. A judgment. They got a copy of the judgment and were appalled, both by the judgment and by the disparity between the true story and what Cooper had led them to believe. Needless to say, they backed out of the deal.

After this couple backed out, Cooper's lawyer called them and asked repeatedly if they talked to us and what we said; he was obviously looking for some excuse to sue us. It probably never occurred to him that the deal fell through because Cooper had not properly fixed the house and had lied.

A similar scenario was repeated two more times over the next few weeks. People who had seen the house and been shown Cooper's letter (presumably before the end of September, 1989) called us. We heard the same story as with the first couple. The nature of the defects and the reason for Cooper owning a vacated house were misrepresented. Cooper said the defects were only minor, confined to one section of the house, and that *everything* had been fixed. No mention of the trial, the legal judgment, or the fact that all three levels of the house — not just the basement area — were proven in court to be structurally defective. On both occasions the interested party sought a copy of the judgment (a matter of public record), read the truth, and backed out.

End of the Story

After our lawyer's letter was mailed and the third potential buyer backed out, the selling strategy changed. In November 1989 the asking price was dropped to $369,000, and we heard no more about Cooper's lies or his outrageous letter. Presumably the letter was discarded in favor of a more honest approach.

In March 1990 Cooper finally sold the house. The buyers made no attempt to contact us. We do not know the selling price or special financing terms, if any, of the deal. Nor do we know if Cooper fixed the house properly before the new owners moved in. If he did, then they should have a lovely home.

*   *   *

In April 1990 we received an unexpected legal bill from Tom's firm for $1900. The document we had signed before the October 1988 trial put us on a contingency arrangement but also obligated us to pay expenses advanced by the law firm in preparation for the trial. The bill was for copying costs, computerized legal searches, and photographs used at trial.

We called Tom. "Why did you wait so long to bill us?"

"I never closed out your case. I just closed your file last

week," Tom answered, adding: "Don't forget, you had forty-five thousand dollars in unbilled legal time. And you didn't get billed for the work I did after the title transferred, all the letters and everything else. I really can't do anything about the nineteen hundred dollars. I'm afraid you have to pay it."

If Tom's claim about the unbilled legal time was correct (and we have no reason to doubt it), the total cost to seek legal redress in a case of obvious and undisputed defective residential construction on a single-family home was $104,000, of which we paid out-of-pocket nearly $60,000. I will leave it to the reader to judge the sanity of our legal system.

Crooked House is Published

People could not believe our story. Mainly, they could not fathom that the law allows a dishonest developer to profit from selling a defective house — twice. Nor, of course, did the outcome make any sense to us.

Make no mistake. The loss of our home and $160,000 because we did business with a sociopathic developer and his incompetent cronies hurt, and will continue to hurt to the end of our days. I hope my story — and all the information that follows — will help protect you and your family from similar pain.

One way we handled our sense of injustice was to write about it. At first I wrote letters to the newspapers and to the town's officials. Then I wrote a short article for Medical Economics, a magazine that publishes pieces by physicians on social and economic issues ("The Judge Called Our Dream House A Fiasco," Medical Economics, January 22, 1990). Many friends and acquaintances saw my article and liked it. Several said it was important that I warn others about the risks of buying or building a defective new house. Not a few suggested I use my training as a psychiatrist to warn others about dealing with "bad people."

My husband and I had long kept detailed notes about the case. In the beginning, of course, we never dreamed of writing a book. Our initial purpose was just to keep the facts straight. Having written all the letters and my published article, writing the book was a natural sequel. *And They Built A Crooked House* was published in the summer of 1991.

Crooked House was positively reviewed in several local and national publications. Below are portions of one review from OHIOANA, a statewide publication on books by Ohio authors. The headline was chosen by the reviewer.

Ineptitude, Dishonesty and Greed

AND THEY BUILT A CROOKED HOUSE by Ruth S. Martin. *Lakeside Press* [Cleveland], 1991.

And They Built A Crooked House is Ruth Martin's retelling of the whole horrific story. Along the way, the reader is confronted with a virtual encyclopedia of ineptitude, dishonesty and greed on the part of almost every so-called professional the couple trusted [and] paid. What the Martins did to deserve this treatment is a question asked repeatedly throughout the book. The answer is nothing except ignore the classic dictum, "Let the buyer beware."

...Shoddy construction is only half the story here. The American system of justice is also taken to task. Legal fees cost the Martins $60,000 and that does not include $45,000 of billable hours their lawyer agreed not to charge them. Keep in mind that in Ohio, legal fees in a contract dispute cannot be recovered. [Author's note: Nor in any other state, to my knowledge.]

Further, the Martins' day in court was delayed by the droves of lawyers involved in the case, and the backlog in the courts. In addition to the psychological toll, each delay increased legal fees and the overall monetary loss. A speedy trial certainly qualifies as an oxymoron.

And They Built a Crooked House is an incredible but not uncommon story. People in the construction industry can regale listeners with stories of similar atrocities. This may not be the most polished read of the year, but it should be required reading for those considering the average person's largest single purchase, a home. (Reviewer: Theodore B. Kinni)

In addition to the reviews, my husband and I were featured in stories that appeared in suburban dailies, and for a while there was intense publicity about the book. Because I changed all the names in the story except ours, including the name of the community, we didn't expect any repercussions from the three defendants.   They had chosen to go to court in a public trial instead of fixing our house, and we had proved material breach of contract, so they could hardly complain about any publicity.

Our legal advice regarding publication was straightforward: because practically everything about the case was a matter of public record, writing about the events and even mentioning the defendants' real names was in no way libelous.   Truth is an absolute defense against libel. However, our kids attend the same public school as the developer's grandchildren, and we had no wish to embarrass his innocent family (or, for that matter, the families of the other participants), so we changed the names.

We also realized that people outside our area wouldn't know Jake Cooper from Adam.   While writing the book we heard or read about construction problems in other states, and it became apparent that our message was not limited to one slice of Ohio. We had something important to tell homebuyers all over the nation.   In the forward to *Crooked House* I wrote: "The men who desecrated our house operate in one small area of one county of this huge country.   This book is really for homeowners and homebuyers everywhere because the problem we experienced — defective residential construction — happens all over.   Who the players were in our particular case is not nearly so important as understanding how this nightmare can happen and how to prevent it."

Section 2. Why you may be out of luck if you buy a defective house — no matter what the contract says. True stories from all over the country

> The upshot of all this is the fact that regardless of the area of the country, shoddy construction goes on all the time right next to excellent construction.
> — Robert Irwin, *Tips and Traps When Buying a Home*, McGraw-Hill, 1990.

What happened to us and our house may be one of the worst individual cases on record, but defective residential construction happens all over the country.

The problem is not as widely appreciated as it should be. No author has taken it upon himself or herself to publish the dark side of home building, the obverse of Tracy Kidder's best selling book *House*. That book chronicles, from concept to move-in, the construction of one single-family home in Massachusetts. Everything went well because the builders were good. That is what everyone hopes for but, unfortunately, it doesn't always happen. Surprisingly, however, I may be the only author who has chronicled what happens when the builders are *bad*.

Although defective construction is a common and widespread problem, it is generally under reported at the national level. There is no national clearinghouse for residential construction disasters, even those that go to trial. Lawyers searching a legal data base for cases involving residential construction would not find ours, because it was not appealed. Only appellate cases are published and therefore retrievable by computer search. (If you know of a specific case you can obtain a copy of the written opinion where the trial took place.)

The information is out there, but it is widely scattered among: hundreds of local newspaper articles, thousands of individual civil

43

lawsuits, the minutes of state legislatures and the U.S. Congress, and the file cabinets of home warranty companies.

I have only reviewed a small fraction of this material, but it is enough to discover a constant theme: if the builder won't fix a major construction problem, the homeowner is out of luck. When the builder reneges the result is aggravation and despair, and often financial hardship. There is no "lemon law" to protect buyers of defective homes. In truth, the American consumer has more protection when buying a refrigerator or television than a new home.

Some Explanations

There are several explanations for this sad situation. First, houses are built by people who are unlicensed in many states, and unregulated in all states. Builders will protest that they are highly regulated, but in fact regulations that exist are so often breached with impunity that they provide no meaningful protection for the homebuyer. About licensing for contractors, William Marchiony wrote in *The New House Buyer's Guide*:

> It is interesting to note that some states, even though they require the licensing of General Contractors, do so only to collect additional state revenue! One would think that if they go to the trouble of setting up the licensing process, they would go the rest of the way and require examinations to test the competency and monitor the ethical conduct of their licensees.

In truth, virtually *anyone* can call himself a contractor and build a house for sale; a license, when it is required, is a mere formality. There are no tests of competency, financial solvency, or even literacy. If the builder is incompetent in structural matters there is no one to stop him or make him correct mistakes once they are made.

Second, many local builders are undercapitalized. They build the next house with profit from the last one. Although several large firms build homes nationwide, custom-construction is usually handled by local contractors, and most of them cannot afford expensive mistakes. When confronted with a construction disaster the local builder may reason that his best course is simply to ignore the complaint (unless he is of unusual integrity). If he is sued and loses in court he can always file bankruptcy, a common practice among builders when they are legally challenged. For most builders bankruptcy is nothing more than a temporary inconvenience until they restructure and come back under a new name. Meanwhile, the home owner has lost everything and has no chance of collecting any legal judgment.

A third reason buyers of defective homes are often out of luck has to do with the nature of the defects. Significant construction problems are seldom functional. Mechanical, electrical, and plumbing systems invariably work in new houses or, if defective, they are apt to be fixed before the homeowner takes possession. Most construction horror stories come from people who, like us, can live in their defective dwelling.

The major disputed problem is usually a structural or design flaw such as sloping floors, bowing walls, a leaky roof or an inadequate foundation. In this situation it is all too easy to dispute a homeowner's complaints ("optical illusion" is what we were told about obviously sloping floors), or blame some other party. It's harder for a builder to argue if something plainly doesn't work; a functional problem will usually be fixed, even if the homeowner has to do it himself. (On occasion during our ordeal someone would comment: "Well, you're living in the house so it can't be that bad," or "The plumbing's working so what are you worried about?")

But if the floors slope or the walls bow or the basement floods or the roof leaks, the builder can dawdle or deny the problem or just blame someone else. Meanwhile the house will be unsalable because of the defects, and the homeowner will see his equity evaporate. Find a major defect that the builder won't fix, and you will find yourself out of luck.

"Cancer Wrapped in Ribbons and Lace"

The home horror stories getting told to the judge

An article under this headline in the September 6, 1987, Atlanta Journal and Constitution, listed several major residential construction disasters in the Atlanta area, including a

> $700,000 house [with] hardwood floors that buckled as a result of improper drainage, sagging ceilings caused by roof leaks, unsafe wiring in the attic...

The article went on to note:

> Horror stories have not become the norm but they are increasing in metropolitan Atlanta... Generally, lawsuits involve more expensive homes and cases involving more than $10,000 in repair costs.
>
> Attorney Anthony Kirkland, who has handled construction cases in several metro counties said, "When [people] buy a $100,000 house and things are not right, they find out they have to hire experts - an architect, appraiser, builder, etc. - to testify on what is wrong." That cost scares them away from litigation, he added.
>
> Jeff Pope, an independent Atlanta house inspector who specializes in luxury homes and properties involved in litigation, is zealous in ferreting out defects that he says can prove to be "cancer wrapped in ribbons and lace." Even in the most expensive homes, he said, builders sometimes put in low grade or defective wood where it will be covered by finishing materials.
>
> ...increasingly, brokers and their agents are encouraging homebuyers to hire private inspectors to check properties, thus relieving some of their liability...

A related story on the same date told of a metropolitan Atlanta couple whose $145,000 home was defectively built in such a way that

> the weight of the house was not properly distributed on its foundation and...joists were of inferior quality or had been damaged during construction.

When their homeowners insurance coverage expired at the end of the first year in their house, they were unable to obtain liability insurance on the house and got structural insurance only through an expensive high-risk policy from a pool of insurance companies.

Last month they moved out of the house when their builder...bought the house back from them as part of a $176,000 settlement of the lawsuit in which they alleged fraud and a house "unsafe to live in." The settlement was reached the day before the case was to go to trial.

Most purchasers of a seriously defective new home are not so lucky as that Atlanta couple. From the Cleveland Plain Dealer, April 3, 1989:

When the [Homeowners] decided in 1986 to build their dream home, they never thought they would be caught in a battle with their builder. But the family said that since...contracting to build their home, they had had so many problems they couldn't enjoy the house.

Highland Heights, where the [Homeowners] live, last year revoked the builder's license...because of residents' complaints about the firm.

"We want our house fixed," [Mr. Homeowner] said. "We just want our children to be able to enjoy what we worked so hard for." [Mr. Homeowner] said he filed suit last month in Cuyahoga County Common Pleas Court as a last resort. The suit seeks the money to repair the home and punitive damages.

"They're not willing to negotiate," the builder said. "They're lying. These people are not reasonable."

Later in this Cleveland article the builder's attorney is quoted:

"People expect perfection in a home, and there is no builder in the world that can build a perfect home."

> Homeowners become emotional and are bound to have small disputes with a builder, he said.
>
> "On a big-ticket purchase like a home, there's always going to be some disputes," he said. "To build a home and have a dispute with the builder is not at all uncommon."

Anyone Can Become a Victim

"Not at all uncommon." A euphemism for "more common than you think." A nightmare with defective construction can happen to anyone, wealthy or middle class, working or retired, married or single. A retired Methodist minister and his wife bought their dream home in the mountains of North Carolina for $90,000. According to a newsletter published in 1991 by the North Carolina Homeowners Association,

> When [the minister and his wife] noticed cracks and bulges in the walls and defects in the flooring, the dream home became their worst nightmare. They found that the house had no footings beneath it and was literally falling off the mountain. They were forced to sell the house for $10,000, the value of the lot alone. They sued the realty company, the original homeowner, and the builder. They lost in trial court. The North Carolina courts did not hold the builder responsible for failing to put a proper foundation under the house. The couple lost $30,000 in lawyer fees and court costs in addition to the $80,000 on the defective house. Those unfortunates who buy a defective house in North Carolina are stuck with it. It's "buyer beware" on the most important investment of your life.

The following is from a January 31, 1992 news release about CBS sportscaster and Superbowl announcer John Madden's multi-million dollar home.

Madden Sues As Home Cracks Up

John Madden, former Oakland Raiders Coach and current football commentator on television, has filed suit claiming his $4.5 million home is riddled with problems. Madden and his wife...claim their 6-year-old home in the exclusive Blackhawk, Calif. community has cracks in the foundation, masonry, doorjambs, interior walls, ceilings and kitchen counters, according to the lawsuit. The suit names 11 contractors, financial firms and others in addition to the Blackhawk Corp. and four related companies. The lawsuit seeks reimbursement of $1.5 million, plus the cost of repairing the house. Exact cost of those repairs has not been determined.

An unusual group of unhappy homeowners was profiled in a Baltimore Sun article that appeared March 2, 1992.

Nuns, contractor in legal tussle over construction

Sister ------- M. is accustomed to putting her faith in God.

But for the next several weeks, she also will be putting her faith in Henry H. Lewis Contractors, Inc.

The Owings Mills-based firm is racing to complete a $3.7 million motherhouse for Sister M. and the religious order she heads, Mission Helpers of the Sacred Heart.

The rush is on because the nuns fired their previous contractor — twice — and are counting on Lewis to help them meet a March 23 deadline for leaving their current home...

The nuns say construction delays and building defects by the first contractor prevented them from moving into the new building. The contractor, --- Builders Inc., says the nuns wanted perfection and interfered with the construction causing the delays.

Now, it's up to a three member arbitration panel to judge who's right.

"They're suing us. We're suing them," said Sister M. "To be quite honest, we were first-time builders and women and nuns on top of that. They must have thought we didn't know what we were doing."

"We trusted," Sister M. said. "We trusted that the [original] contractors were looking out for us, and they weren't. We've been living out of boxes

> for eight months now because we thought our
> building would be finished. We get ready to move
> and think we're going to move and then we don't
> move. It's psychological torture. Mental anguish."
>
> ...An attorney for [the nuns' original builders] said
> the firm "bent over backward to satisfy the sisters —
> but to no avail."
>
> "They're nuns," he said. I believe because of
> their lack of construction experience...and the
> nature of what they are all about, they are probably
> impossible to please."

The Baltimore article goes on to detail the exact nature of the construction disputes. Two things are abundantly clear from this story. The nuns' motherhouse was originally designed and/or constructed in a sloppy and unprofessional manner (pictures show this); and, the *nuns* are blamed for the problems.

Now we turn to a young doctor and his wife, who contracted to build an expensive new home in a Detroit suburb. After they moved in, he wrote an article about their house-building experience. The article was published in the January 20, 1992 issue of Medical Economics, under the headline: **Build your own home? I've got three words of advice. Don't do it.**

What prompted this doctor to such a feverish pitch of advice? He starts the article with words that seem to leave the door ajar for people who would build their own house.

> We know now that building is not for us — nor
> for most people. But if you're going to do it, take
> charge. It's your house and your money, so don't
> let the "experts" tell you what you want.

Under headings such as "The fiasco starts with the architect," "Construction delays become the norm," and "It takes four months to get 92 new windows," he details unending frustration with an unreliable architect, incompetent builders, and contracts and promises that practically everyone breaks. He finally had to dump his original builder and architect, and hire new ones.

The story is brief but the message is universal: expect lots of mistakes and much misfortune unless you hire or deal with the right people. The unhappy author doesn't state the total cost overrun on the house or their outlay for legal fees, but implies it was a bundle. This sadder but wiser doctor ends his article with advice even more pessimistic than my own:

> If a gorgeous lot or a freshly cleared subdivision beckons to you to build your own home, remember my three words. "Don't do it."

In January 1992 a housewife from Maryland wrote me a long, sad letter, detailing the "terror" of a defective new house that both the builder and the homeowner warranty company refused to fix. Included with the letter was an April 17, 1989 article about their plight, from The Frederick Post.

> [The couple] noticed that draperies and pictures hung crooked no matter how they turned them after they moved into their new modular house.
> As the couple and their three daughters settled [in their new home] in October 1987, their list of cosmetic and structural problems grew surprisingly long...Since then, the family has been battling the builder of their home. Meanwhile, Frederick County [Maryland] officials have halted all building permits for the company, and, in addition, the state Attorney General's office is considering legal action.
> ...[The couple] found serious structural faults which appeared to be at the root of the cosmetic problems...Their basement lacks the proper number of columns; exterior siding was not secured properly, and one section of the house seems to be leaning toward the street, they say.
> "You might say we goofed a little bit, but then again those are modular homes," [official] admitted, saying that his department made a mistake in granting an occupancy permit for the home.
> The consumer protection division of the Maryland Attorney General's office has been working on the case for several months, as well...an investigator with the Attorney General's consumer protection division said, "My feeling...is that [the building company] should replace the house."

This was in April 1989. The next three years proved to be an unrelenting nightmare for the homeowners. Their trial date was postponed several times, and they suffered a change in attorneys. Their first attorney sued them for legal fees even though he had taken the case on a contingency basis. To make matters worse, the husband of the woman who wrote me, a career military officer, was transferred out of state. She was unable to join him because they could not sell their house in its defective condition; like most people, they don't have the money to own two houses.

In January 1992 she wrote:

> We had a hydraulic jack supporting the middle of our house for about 2 years. One day the jack failed — and the 6 x 6 post above it fell over onto the basement floor. I wouldn't let the kids into the basement for a long time after that.
> ...The persecution doesn't seem to end — and faceless corporate entities — Greed!   What is the best way to productively deal with something like this?   It isn't just robbing us of our money, but our _time_, our dreams, our happiness, everything.   It's hard to see around it when we're trapped in this cage.

Another Maryland couple was profiled in an article titled "Joys And Perils Of That Unbuilt House," Changing Times Magazine, June 1990.

> Buying a not-yet-built home isn't like buying an existing one. It's harder.
> [Homeowners] learned that lesson almost four years ago, when they entered into a contract to build a four-bedroom colonial in Gambrills, Md. The house took 18 months to complete, almost three times longer than average. Two years after [they] moved in, they are still trying to get the house finished to their liking. At one point, the list of

items they thought their builder should fix was a full page long. Some items were minor...but many, like a persistent water-line leak, were major. Cedar siding damaged during construction was replaced with unstained boards. They had to completely resod the lawn...

And [these people] are smart buyers. She's a real estate agent; he works for a large developer. But the couple say today that they bought because of the location of the development and without investigation. The builder, they have learned, has a reputation for slighting follow-up repairs. And being in a booming market, [they] knew the builder could easily resell the house if they broke their contract. So they hung on, but not without permanently altering their view of the process. Says [Mrs. Homeowner]: "I would never buy another new home."

A doctor, a media star, a retired minister, a housewife, a real estate agent, a group of nuns — all with the same problem. Are they all so stupid that they don't know how to buy or contract for a properly-constructed house? Of course not. They are a microcosm of all the innocent victims of defective residential construction in this country. *Anyone* can be become a victim. From Maine to California, from Alaska to Hawaii, everyone is at risk when building or buying a new house. Including you.

Where Are The Inspectors?

Every buyer of a defective new home asks the same question: how did my house pass inspection? Most inspectors are local government employees, hired by the city or town to assure that new construction is fit for occupancy. When the house passes inspection the homebuyer is given an official 'occupancy permit'. Yet defective houses — houses not built in accordance with local building codes — commonly pass inspection.

How does this happen? There are several reasons, and they vary from place to place, indeed from house to house. Proceeding from the most benign to the criminal, reasons defective houses pass inspection include the following:

1) The defects are hidden so that no typical house inspector could expect to find them on a routine inspection. The defects only become apparent over time, after the homeowners have moved in.

2) The inspector is overworked. Because of a large number of new houses, and an inadequate number of inspectors, each inspector only has time to check basic systems, e.g., electrical, heating, and plumbing. The inspector does the best job he can in a limited amount of time.

3) The inspector is not competent for the task. He has no special knowledge about house construction and doesn't know what to look for, so he misses obvious defects.

4) The inspector is lazy; he signs off on the house without actually inspecting it.

5) The inspector moonlights for the builder when not working for the community. Depending on local laws, this 'extra work' may or may not be illegal. Regardless, the inspector is not about to bite the hand that feeds him.

6) The inspector is under pressure from his superiors to either approve a house or risk losing his job. The inspection department functions as a "rubber stamp" for the local builders.

7) The inspector knows the house is defective, but is paid by the builder or developer to lie and issue a permit.

One would like to think that the only reason defective houses pass inspection is number 1. Unfortunately, that is not so. In fact, considering all the cases that have come to my attention, hidden defects — those that cannot be uncovered on a final, thorough inspection — is probably the least common reason. A far more prevalent reason, it seems, is that inspectors just don't have the expertise, or are not given enough time, to do an adequate job.

A review of the problem in North Carolina appeared in the Charlotte Observer on March 17, 1990. After detailing cases of defective construction that had passed inspection, the article noted:

> In each of the examples given in this story, local inspectors approved the new houses for occupancy...[The chief building inspector for Charlotte said] his building inspectors must check about three houses an hour — a house every 20 minutes, not including travel time between houses. "We feel we're doing adequate inspections," he said. "We'd prefer to have more time, obviously."
>
> When inspectors find code violations in a house they've already approved, there's usually little they can do. A few local governments deny builders new permits until they correct code violations.
>
> But most local governments will issue permits to a builder even if he or she has code violations on other houses. It takes an ordinance passed by the local council or commissioners to allow inspectors to withhold permits until other code problems are fixed.

It is not clear why the inspector quoted in this article feels his men can do an adequate job in only 20 minutes. In any case, according to James R. Parker, President of the North Carolina Homeowners Association, the law in his state actually requires an inspector to "make as many inspections as necessary to ensure compliance with the state building code." Mr. Parker notes that "Inspectors might feel as if they must inspect a home in a certain time frame (because of political pressure), but State law dictates that they take as much time as required to adequately perform that inspection."

A realistic appraisal of the consequences of short inspection times was provided in an Atlanta Journal and Constitution article from September 6, 1987:

> County building officials don't claim to be doing an adequate job. Given the large number of inspections, [the] chief residential inspector in Cobb

County said his five full-time and one part-time inspectors "are allowed about 10 minutes per call." For instance on one day late in August the inspectors averaged 27 inspections each. The Southern Building Code Congress, whose uniform codes are followed in Cobb and other metro counties, recommends a maximum workload of 12 to 14 inspections per day.

[The chief inspector] of Fulton county is trying to hire 10 inspectors that are needed to get the department to the bare minimum of performance. With inspectors averaging almost 11 inspections per day, he noted, "there is not enough time to do the best we can do."

Inadequate inspections is a nationwide problem with new construction. And the results are devastating everywhere. The following excerpts are from a 1989 story in the Ft. Lauderdale News (italics added):

[Homeowner] said that when his home was completed in June 1987, he was obligated under his contract to close on the property because the building department had issued a certificate of occupancy...*The certificate was issued despite a list he compiled of 17 noticeable flaws*... [Homeowner] blames [Builder] for a poor construction job and the city's building department...for issuing a certificate of occupancy without checking to see if the house was fit to live in. [The building inspector] did not return repeated calls from the Fort Lauderdale News and Sun Sentinel.

Among the problems: an uneven tile roof, a kitchen floor that had flooded, a garage that floods every time it rains, a crack along one side of the outside wall, a crooked inside wall and a ruined $5,000 black awning streaked with white paint.

An independent company hired by [Homeowner] last year inspected the property and issued a report detailing 38 flaws that would take $56,370 to repair.

Another article in the Ft. Lauderdale Sun-Sentinel, from August 9, 1989, discussed the structural problems in some houses that are sinking because they were built over a canal filled with rubbish (italics added).

> No one can explain why the canal was allowed to be filled with rubbish or how a developer was able to build homes there. [Homeowner] said the problems at his home greatly increased in 1976, when an 11-acre lake about 50 yards away was dredged... Now the same developer...wants to dredge the lake again...Residents...said that if the town grants another dredging permit, their homes will be destroyed.
>
> [Homeowner] said he spent $25,000 to repair the home. He raised the back end by a foot and poured 46 truckloads of fill into the back yard to even it out.
>
> After discovering that the homes were built on a landfill he sued the town for issuing the building permits, but the *suit was thrown out of court*. It was determined that the town followed procedures in effect at the time.

Can inspectors who pass on defective construction be held legally responsible? No. Homeowners are unprotected because local governments, and their representatives, are immune from lawsuits over defective construction. Housing inspectors who let pass defective construction may be criticized or embarrassed, or on occasion even fired, but that's as far as it goes; they *and* the local government are legally protected by the doctrine of "sovereign immunity." Lawsuits like the one quoted above are routinely "thrown out of court."

From an article in the Richmond Times-Dispatch, February 22, 1992, reporting on defective construction in that area of Virginia.

Owners Demanding Better Inspections

...And in Chesterfield County, several homeowners with cracked foundations are baffled because, they say, the same county inspection system that didn't protect them is now protecting the builders who put up their homes. Their houses were give a certificate of occupancy, the county's seal of approval.

Builders can use that "CO" as proof that everything was done right, even in cases where independent engineers have found code violations that were missed by the county inspectors. The homeowners say they've been left holding the bag.

Are there conflicts of interest among inspectors? You have to wonder. The following excerpts are from an editorial in the Frederick Post (Maryland), May 14, 1991:

...Some county employees — inspectors — may have been moonlighting. That doesn't sound too bad, because a lot of county employees, trying to make ends meet, get part-time jobs. But according to one Frederick County commissioner, the inspectors who are moonlighting are working in the very industry in which they are inspecting.

Now this is kind of hard to believe. Can we assume that someone goes out to inspect a construction site, for example, says it's wonderful, and then we discover that the same person is also working on that site? It would be like the inspector is inspecting his own work. Bet it passes inspection.

...County inspectors should not also be working for the very people they are inspecting. Period.

Do some inspectors sign off on houses without actually inspecting them? Apparently so. An example of that practice came to light in a large lawsuit filed by a group of 34 California homeowners (see page 134).

Condominiums

One might think that builders and developers are more responsive to a large condominium project, where dozens of homeowners can generate more clout than just one. That is not necessarily so. There seem to be just as many horror stories from condominium owners as from owners of single family dwellings. The following is from the Miami Herald, February 18, 1990.

Condominium owners want builder to pay for repairs

Tired of an unsettled dispute with a developer over what they claim are construction defects in their condominium near Hallandale, a group of owners took their protest to the streets.

They put up a sign on the grounds of the 88-unit condominium, telling the world about their woes.

"I want to go further," said [one unit owner]. "I think we should picket."

...other condo owners detailed numerous problems: leaks in ceilings, rotting garage doors, cracks in doorways, sloping bathtubs, peeling pain and beige facades that turned dark because they weren't treated for mildew.

"It's been a financial hardship," said [homeowner], who has been living at the condo since it opened in 1986. "We're a young couple and we bought new so we wouldn't have all these things."

Condo board president...said, "We've had to assess our people twice already because we could not live with the problems. Buildings that were a year and a half old looked like they were 50 years old."

The Miami Herald article goes on to mention how there have been "two years of negotiations" and "the attorneys are dealing with it."

The July 15, 1990 Ft. Lauderdale Sun-Sentinel published a page one article headlined

Condo industry crumbling

The door is slamming shut on the carefree lifestyle at many South Florida condos.

Mismanagement, shoddy construction and lax regulation threaten to cost condominium boards

thousands of dollars and are prompting a spate of
lawsuits and foreclosures.

The article goes on to document the thousands of
condominium complaints filed each year in South Florida, most
based on shoddy construction. Many condominium owners in that
part of the country are experiencing the same aggravations and
nightmarish expenses we had with our single-family home.

South Florida has been riddled with complaints about
condominium construction. In the last few years hardly a month
goes by without some article in a South Florida newspaper
pointing out the nightmares of defective construction.   The
following article appeared in the Ft. Lauderdale Sun-Sentinel,
May 24, 1991.

Homeowners file suit

Eighty homeowners in the [Development]
community in south Dade County filed suit against
[----] Homes on Thursday, charging that the
company used untreated wood and non-galvinized
steel in the construction of their homes during the
late 1980s.

The suit, which alleges breach of contract, breach
of warranty and negligence was filed in Dade
Circuit Court.   Ervin Gonzalez, lawyer for the
plaintiffs, estimated that damages could reach as
much as $25,000 per home.

He said [the company], recently ranked 16th in a
survey of the nation's largest builders, offered to
repair porches in a few of the affected homes but
left other repairs related to rust and wood rot to the
responsibility of homeowners.

Construction problems with condominiums are not confined to
South Florida, of course. From the Denver Post, October 9, 1989
(reporting a problem in Aurora, Colorado):

A builder who built a cluster of condos a decade
ago that still produces complaints of shoddy
workmanship from unit owners is facing those angry
owners in a zoning dispute over whether he should

be allowed to build again before settling those grievances. Since 1979, residents of the [----- Condos] have struggled with flooded basements, peeling paint and crumbling retaining walls in the 33-unit project by [Builder].

"We've been fighting with the builder since the day we moved in," said the president of the homeowner's association. "I feel like he owes us something. He should either buy the units back from us or get them so they're impervious to water."

The Aurora, Colorado article goes on to detail the dispute with the builder. As in most disputes we've heard or read about, the builder denies responsibility. But so does the community. The article quotes the Aurora building inspector:

"I can verify that that roof is put on the way the city-approved drawing says. But the uniform building code does not cover workmanship. The builders come in and they build strictly minimum standards."

The Seville Place Fiasco

Perhaps no situation has been more frustrating for condominium owners, or received more media attention, than Seville Place in North Dade, Florida, just northwest of Miami. Seville Place has been the subject of several TV documentaries, countless newspaper and magazine articles, and at least one Congressional Hearing. What exactly happened at Seville Place?

Seville Place is a condominium project of "tropical, fruit-colored townhomes" constructed between 1986 and 1989. The homes cost between $70,000 and $90,000, and many of the mortgages were backed by the Federal Housing Authority. Seventy of the units were built by Hoffman Homes of Itasca, Illinois, and most of these were guaranteed by the Homeowners Warranty Corporation, a builder-sponsored company that issues *structural insurance* on new houses and condominiums. HOW issued a "10-year warranty on the units."

Shortly after the owners took possession, many defects began appearing: leaky roofs, walls disconnected to the slab floors, water pouring out of electrical outlets, etc. Several detailed inspections were made of the entire structure, including one by the Dade County Commissioners. Their finding: *"The walls are not sufficiently strong to support the upper stories in a stiff wind."* In other words, the units were not built to withstand south Florida hurricanes and therefore, by local building standards, were considered unsafe to inhabit! The homeowners were ordered to fix the problem or *face eviction.* The story played heavily in the South Florida newspapers. The following item is from the Ft. Lauderdale Sun-Sentinel, May 24, 1991.

GONE WITH THE WIND

...As hurricane season approaches, residents find themselves in housing that falls well below local hurricane standards. And the county [Dade] has ordered the homes demolished

Now, young professional couples find themselves in the middle of a legal quagmire, living in homes that are both unsafe and impossible to sell

Instead of building on their equity, they find themselves spending their life savings trying to salvage something from a real estate nightmare.

How did this happen? Again, quoting local newspapers:

The design flaw, the result of mathematical miscalculations, left the walls unsafe in winds stronger than 80 mph...Building and zoning official Ron Szep said the county relies largely on a self-inspection system by engineers selected by a developer. But in this case, that system wasn't enough...The Dade Board of Rules and Appeals recently rewrote the portion of the South Florida Building Code covering special inspectors like the one hired to oversee construction of Seville Place. But Florida legislators say more needs to be done on the federal level to ensure that FHA-backed projects like Seville Place are properly inspected during construction.

"This project should never have been signed off on," said U.S. Rep Larry Smith, D-Hollywood.

Meanwhile, according to articles in the Miami Herald, the cost to properly reinforce the Seville Place units was $1.7 million. The homeowners were in no position to pay this amount. What about their HOW policy, which had warranted to repair structural defects? HOW refused to make the repairs, arguing that "the defect was not covered because no actual damage had occurred."

A lawsuit was filed against HOW, and the homeowners began incurring thousands of dollars in legal fees, $200,000 by the time of settlement according to one newspaper article. The case garnered media attention because of the number of families involved, the Dade County eviction order, the apparent refusal of the insurer to make good on its policy and, not least, because several prominent politicians became involved. In 1991 Congress held a hearing on the government's responsibility insofar as the structurally-defective property was backed by FHA-guaranteed mortgages. Several Seville Place home owners testified.

Faced with intense media pressure, and direct intervention by Senators Connie Mack and Robert Graham of Florida, an out-of-court settlement was finally reached in late 1991. Although terms of the agreement were not publicly disclosed, an attorney for the Seville Place homeowners was quoted as saying "the money will be sufficient to repair all 70 townhouses."

Hurricane Andrew, which devastated much of South Florida in August 1992, showed what can happen when construction is less than it should be. In Andrew's wake were thousands of demolished homes that had *not been built to code*. A typical story about the problem, from the Ft. Lauderdale Sun-Sentinel August 28, 1992, began:

Slipshod building: a disaster

Shoddy home construction and widespread violations of the Dade County building code greatly increased the devastation caused by Hurricane Andrew, building experts said this week.

Structural engineers who inspected the remains of homes in Andrew's wake said many of the houses that were destroyed would have survived without significant damage had they been built in accordance with the code.

It is obviously better to learn of shoddy construction before a hurricane like Andrew hits. But if you then become entangled in a legal and financial quagmire, you will have a nightmare experience even in calm weather. Quotes from two homeowners during the Seville Place battle: "The systems of controls failed. It was a full melt-down;" and, "To many of us, this was our life savings. Now we cannot legally transfer title. Some people have had to turn down job offers to move."

One of the Seville Place homeowners active in the case wrote the following letter to the Miami Herald (published over his name on December 7, 1991).

> I am one of the homeowners who took a very active role in getting the message across of the enormous tragedy that was being played out with 70 innocent homeowners. I was invited to testify in Washington, D.C. before a congressional sub-committee on Banking, Housing and Urban Affairs.
>
> Throughout this nightmare I learned a lot about politicians and what they can do to help a cause. After writing dozens of letters to county, state, and federal politicians, I soon realized the meaning of lip service. Most politicians turned the other way and ran as fast as they could.
>
> However, there were some exceptions. The two most vocal and active were Metro Commissioner Mary Collins and U.S. Senator Connie Mack. Senator Mack...has introduced legislation to prevent such a tragedy from happening to other homeowners...

You can sense the frustration this writer and the other condo owners felt during their long ordeal. But consider the facts in this particular case. Dozens of homeowners. A major lawsuit. Intense publicity. A hearing before the U.S. Congress. Active intervention by several high ranking politicians. *Only then* was there a settlement.

What chance does the average condominium owner have of making builders and insurers correct structural defects, if the defects don't draw much attention of the press and politicians? I can tell you. Very little.

What About Homeowner Warranties?

Many builders offer third party warranties for new construction. The oldest of these policies is issued by the Home Owner's Warranty Corp. (HOW), of Arlington, VA. HOW was one of the defendants in the Seville Place litigation.

In the early 1970s Congress was considering regulating home builders because of numerous complaints about construction defects. In response, HOW was set up by the National Association of Home Builders in 1974 to "insure American home-buyers against defects in their new homes and also against any negative consequences form the bankruptcy of the builder who put it up" (Mayer 1978).

HOW is one of three nationwide companies offering builder-sponsored new-home warranties. The two others are Residential Warranty Corp. of Harrisburg, PA and Home Buyers Warranty of Denver, the nation's largest such company.

Builder-offered warranties supposedly insure against structural defects discovered within the new house's first 10 years. The policies can only be purchased through the builder, and the cost is passed on to the homeowner (either directly or built into the cost of the home). We had never heard of such policies when we built our house, as none of the local builders in our area seemed to offer them. When we did learn of their existence, it was long after our case had gone to court. Why, we wondered, didn't our builder offer us this policy? At first we thought such a policy would have protected us from the nightmare of litigation that ensued. Now, we're not so sure.

It turns out that HOW and similar policies often *do not* recognize or pay for major structural mistakes. In the last few years it has become apparent that these insurance policies are very limited, and that the companies behind them might refuse to honor what, to the homeowner, looks like a legitimate claim. As a result, there have been numerous lawsuits against the companies that issue the warranties.

The cases of the Maryland family (page 51) and of Florida's Seville Place Condominiums (page 61) are but two of several involving home warranty companies that have recently received publicity. A few other well-publicized cases deserve mention,

from Texas, Virginia, and Washington.   In 1990 a jury in San
Antonio ordered Homeowners Warranty Corp. to pay a
homeowner $483,000 for a home that was falling apart because of
a crack in the foundation.   Of this amount, $325,000 was for
punitive damages, something almost unheard of in the annals of
construction litigation.

In September 1991 a Virginia federal appeals court handed
down a ruling ordering Home Buyers Warranty to abide by an
earlier arbitrator's award of $206,605 for a McLean, VA couple
whose new house was structurally defective. According to a story
in the Washington Post (H. Jane Lehman, "Home Warranty
Policies Coming Under Attack," November 5, 1991), "the
foundation was designed for a one-story house, not the three
stories actually built atop it." The couple living in the house had
achieved some notoriety because of a huge hole they had dug in
their front yard. The hole was necessary in order to

> fix the foundation when neither the builder nor
> their homeowner's warranty company responded to
> an engineer's report that found that the front of the
> house was in danger of collapsing because of the
> inadequately built foundation.
>
> ...Ultimately [the couple] prevailed, winning a
> $206,605 federal appeals court judgment this month
> against Denver-based National Home Insurance
> Co., the insurer behind their Home Buyers warranty
> (HBW) coverage. The award covered the [couple's]
> hefty bill for the 1989 foundation repairs, which they
> paid themselves pending the outcome of their fight
> with HBW.
>
> [This couple's] case is one of a growing number
> of lawsuits that have filed across the country against
> companies offering 10-year warranties against faulty
> home construction. The suits have accused the
> insurance firms of deceptive trade practices, fraud
> and racketeering in refusing to honor what the
> homeowners contend are legitimate claims.
>
> A year ago, the American Trial Lawyers
> Association formed a litigation group to compare
> notes on the homeowner warranty cases. While
> plaintiffs' attorneys see a pattern of failure within

the warranty industry to honor its legal obligations, officials for the companies contend that the suits are indicative of widespread misunderstanding as to what the warranties actually cover.

Perhaps the most incredible home warranty case I've come across involves a couple in Bellevue, Washington. Their $250,000 HOW-insured new home developed a crack in the garage floor shortly after they moved in. According to an article on homeowners warranties in Kiplinger's Personal Finance Magazine ("Homeowners warranties: Cracks in the coverage," April 1992), the builder patched the crack, but it reappeared. The builder patched it again. When the crack appeared once more, the builder told the couple to turn to their HOW policy for further repairs. Even though two teams of engineers pronounced the crack a major structural defect, HOW said the crack didn't qualify as a major defect under the policy. When that crack widened and others appeared, the couple sued HOW. Ultimately the city of Bellevue *condemned* the house and the couple had to move out. What exactly was the problem? According to the article,

> [The house] had been built on uncompacted fill dirt, and there were no footings or steel reinforcements in the poured-concrete foundation. Some of the pilings for the garage were either sitting on dirt or, as [homeowner] describes it, "just hanging in midair."
> ...Three days before the start of the trial in state superior court, HOW signed an agreement to pay for fixing the house and to cover all out-of-pocket expenses. HOW signed a construction contract and a HOW-approved contractor was in the process of tearing down part of the house when HOW decided it didn't like the size of the price tag and reneged on its agreement to pay. Now the couple are suing HOW in federal court with a tab for legal fees and repairs running close to $1.2 million.

The Kiplinger article goes on to discuss problems with homeowner warranties in general.

Homeowners who have taken warranty companies to court have also discovered that there's little screening of builders and few controls on construction quality: HOW had only 12 people nationwide to review more than one million homes last year. Adding to homeowners misery are what the Department of Housing and Urban Development has called the unreasonable delays and hardball tactics of the warranty companies in responding to claims.

...The bottom line, says Ernie F. Roberts, a Cornell University law professor, is that the warranties are not intended to protect consumers. They're designed to protect builders from open-ended liability.

Another review of the situation appeared in the Wall Street Journal September 19, 1991, in an article by Milo Geyelin titled "Home Buyer-Warranty Firm Cases Rise."

With buyers of new homes turning increasingly to insurers to protect them against shoddy construction, plaintiffs lawyers are raising concern about whether policyholders have been getting their money's worth.

..."The problem with a lot of these warranties is that everyone who buys a house thinks they're covered, and a lot of times they're not," said Marina Corodemus, a plaintiffs' lawyer in Perth Amboy, N.J., who has begun an information exchange network for similar complaints through the Association of Trial Lawyers of America, the national plaintiffs' lawyers group. "Homebuyers end up holding the bag at the point where the builders have bailed out," she said.

Obviously, the worst cases make the newspapers and magazines. But the 'worst case' is what all these homeowners thought they were insured against. Cases like these prompted a 1991 Congressional hearing on the subject, before the House subcommittee on housing and community development. Only a few of the victims gave testimony, and to date no definite legislation has been proposed to remedy the problem. At the hearing Juan Acosta, a deputy assistant secretary of the Housing and Urban Development Department, testified that "warranty companies [often] unreasonably delay claim payments, or claims adjusters use high-pressure tactics."

Regarding one of the victims who attended the hearing, the Washington Post wrote (November 5, 1991):

> ...a Fredericksburg [VA] homeowner who observed the hearing, said he, too, has had his share of warranty problems. The roof of his new home of nearly a year has spouted six leaks, the crumbling basement floor floods regularly and the floors are uneven, he said.
>
> [Homeowner] said he rejected HBW's $800 settlement offer because estimates he has received put the repair costs at more than $15,000. "Somebody needs to regulate [the industry] or else we have got to put a stop to it," he said.
>
> After hearing the litany of homeowners' complaints, subcommittee Chairman Henry B. Gonzalez (D-Tex.) said, "I cannot begin to tell you how worrisome and demoralizing all this is."

One attorney experienced in home warranty litigation is Bernard DiMuro, of Alexandria, VA, chairman of a special committee on homeowners warranty litigation of the American Trial Lawyers Association. Mr. DiMuro, who won the $206,605 appeals case, is frequently quoted about home warranty cases. According to a December 29, 1991 column in the Washington Post by Jane Bryant Quinn ("Homeowners Build Case Against Warranty Firms"),

> DiMuro has inspected 16 home-warranty complaints filed with the Office of Consumer Affairs in Rockville (MD). He found many homeowners settling for less or just giving up, after months of frustrating correspondence with the insurer.

Just what *do* these new-home warranties cover? Ms. Quinn's column offers some insight:

> Even the 10-year coverage is far more limited than
> it sounds. You're protected only against defects in
> load-bearing structures that render the house
> "unsafe, unsanitary or otherwise unlivable."
> Translation: To collect, your house practically has
> to be falling down around you.

Obviously, the warranty companies do not see things the same
way as homeowner plaintiffs and their lawyers.   From Mr.
Geyelin's WSJ article of September 19, 1991:

> Terrence Cooke, corporate counsel for
> Homeowners Warranty, denied that his company or
> others in the industry attempt in any way to evade
> their responsibility to pay valid claims. As in any
> area of insurance, policyholders must read their
> policies carefully before maintaining that they have
> a claim, he said...

And a few paragraphs from an article by H. Jane Lehman that
appeared in New York Newsday, December 14, 1991:

> Terrence S. Cooke, HOW counsel, denied that his
> company attempts to refuse large claims on flimsy
> grounds or draw out the process to wear down
> homeowners. He said the company has paid more
> than $300 million in claims in 17 years.
> The warranty companies acknowledge they take
> a narrow view of their contractual responsibilities,
> particularly regarding structural defects.   [An
> attorney] for National Home Insurance, which backs
> another national program, Home Buyers Warranty,
> said structural-defects coverage is "designed as
> catastrophic coverage to cover the worst
> possibilities" as determined by a company-paid
> structural engineer.
> "As much as HOW might like to write coverage
> as broadly as some have suggested to cover
> absolutely anything that goes wrong in a house, the
> cost of the policy would be thousand of dollars
> rather than hundreds," Cooke said.

So there it is. Despite the fact that builder-sponsored policies supposedly cover structural defects, their interpretation (by the company) is very narrow. If you can live in your house, and it is not falling down, the warranty company may not admit a claim. More to the point, structural defects that make your house unsalable may not be covered by these policies. If you buy builder-sponsored structural insurance, you need to be aware of its limitations.

The Law Is Stacked Against You

In the preface to the 1984 edition of his book *How to Avoid the Ten Biggest Home-Buying Traps*, A.M. Watkins wrote:

> A few years ago the United States Senate subcommittee on housing held hearings in Washington, D.C., on the subject of defective housing and what could be done to protect homebuyers from bad houses. [I] was asked to testify. To any experienced observer of the housing industry it seemed as if history were repeating itself, for most of the problems aired at the hearings — poor heating, wet basements, shoddy design, and so on — were the very same problems that had caused trouble for homebuyers in the past and have continued to cause trouble in the years since. Such problems form a pattern, and the realization of this fact prompted this book.

In a chapter of the book titled "The Vanishing Builder," Mr. Watkins commented:

> The vanishing builder usually has little or no fear of the law. The law, in fact, has by and large proved ineffectual with such builders. That means most district attorneys, other public officials or agencies, the FHA, the VA, and anybody else you might think could help. All of these people are by law concerned only with criminal violations. To nail a recalcitrant builder, they need clear evidence of fraud. This is often tough to get, or so they say. As a result, the typical district attorney may listen to your woes sympathetically but in the end give you the rush-off. He's dreadfully sorry, he will say, but it's so darned hard to

proved fraud. Patting you on the back in consolation he
leads you to the door, he'll say that you'll have to hire a
lawyer and take the case to civil court. However, help for
home buyers should come soon, since consumer advocates
(like Ralph Nader) will almost certainly turn their attention to
housing.

Watkins's assessment was true in the early 1980s and is true
today.   Unfortunately, it seems that buyers of defective
construction are as unprotected by the legal system as they have
ever been.   While several strong advocates for the rights of
homeowners have emerged, the law remains stacked heavily
against buyers of defective construction. Why so?

Before answering this question let me digress a bit. This book
is mainly about building or buying a new house or condo, but the
problems are pretty much the same when repairing or remodeling
an existing house.   In researching material for this book I
repeatedly came across horror stories about people who hired
remodelers, plumbers, electricians, roofers, etc., and ended up
victimized, swindled, or defrauded of thousands of dollars.

In fact, complaints about home repair and remodeling
consistently ranks number one among categories of consumer
complaint, as compiled by the government. Year after year many
more people repair or remodel their existing homes than buy a
new one, and thus more people are exposed to potentially shoddy
remodeling than to defective new construction.   The problems
have reached such endemic proportion that some states are
setting up funds to reimburse ripped off homeowners. From the
New York Times, March 24, 1991, in a story titled "Recourse for
Shoddy Work":

> At least five states — Arizona, Connecticut,
> Hawaii, Maryland and Virginia — have set up funds
> that reimburse a consumer who can prove he was
> victimized by a contractor's ineptitude or bad faith.
> ...Such plans are needed, several consumer
> protection officials said, because a homeowner who
> wins a court battle against a contractor often cannot
> collect.

Although many of the complaints about home repair and remodeling stem from outright fraud, the vast majority have the same root cause as complaints about defective new construction: bad people doing a bad job. For victims of defective home repair/remodeling *and* defective new-house construction, the law works — or doesn't work — the same way. The homeowner victim has no meaningful legal redress.

Why not?

There are two principal reasons why the law is heavily stacked against consumers of defective new construction or repair: First, business contracts are unenforceable without the expenditure of a large amount of money for lawyers and litigation. Second, in any legal action regarding dispute over a contract, either written or implied, the amount awarded or otherwise recouped by the plaintiff will almost never equal the cost of repairs plus the victim's legal expenses. Again, this is true whether you are a victim of defective construction of a new house or defective repair of an existing home.

The July 15, 1990 Ft. Lauderdale Sun-Sentinel article on condominiums, excerpted earlier, points out that:

> Even if a condo board sues a developer and wins,
> it usually cannot force the other side to pay its legal
> fees, a major cost.

So even if homeowners subject themselves to the tremendous aggravation and expense of filing suit and getting to trial, it is almost impossible to recoup losses or come out financially whole.

From the Medical Economics article by the Detroit doctor:

> By July we were 11 months into our nine-month
> construction plan. The contractor ignored our
> penalty clause, saying it was null because the delays
> were caused by ourselves and the architect...

Later, after the original contractor, Ace Construction, bowed out, Ace put a lien on the doctor's house for

> tens of thousands of dollars in unpaid
> compensation. We countersued for breach of

> contract and damages for the additional cost of
> finishing the house, and the monthly interest
> payments on the construction loan.
>
> ...Two days before the trial, we settled with Ace
> rather than go to court. We got none of the
> damages we asked for and had to pay Ace's
> attorney's fees, as well as our own. But we didn't
> pay any of Ace's bills.

In this case the building contractor reneged on the contract,
then sued for more money. The doctor ended up paying the legal
fees for both sides!

The moment you have to resort to the legal system for redress
on a contract case, you've lost. Your new house requires another
$30,000 to properly finish and Builder X refuses to help? Expect
to spend $10,000 before you have any chance of getting Builder
X to make any offer whatsoever (if then).

Suppose you learn of your house's defects only after you take
possession, that is, after title transfers.   Homes in good
neighborhoods go up in value. Since it takes years to litigate a
major dispute, the value of the home (properly built) would
invariably be higher at the time of trial than when it was
purchased, yet the law doesn't recognize this fact. It costs a
fortune to bring a builder into court; the law doesn't recognize
your expenses. It costs money to "prove" defects; the law doesn't
care about this either.

And suppose you win a judgment? A legal judgment against
a builder or developer is not worth much if the defendant cannot
or will not pay. He can declare bankruptcy, in which case the
homeowner is out of luck. Or the builder can simply ignore the
judgment, which will then require the victimized homeowner to
incur *more* legal expenses in an attempt to find and attach assets.
Builders who don't pay a legal judgment aren't stupid. Debtors
don't go to jail. And chances are you, the luckless plaintiff, won't
find many assets to attach.

Certainly if the builder is truly bankrupt we can't fault the law.
But in many situations the *builder's corporation that constructed the
house is bankrupt,* and the "bankrupt" builder goes right on
building *under a different name.* The following excerpt is from a

November 10, 1991 article in the Los Angeles Times, about shoddy construction around the nation.

> ...shoddy builders often disband their company and form another one to avoid paying claims on defects — which range from dangerous lapses such as undersized electrical wiring and weak foundations to annoying and potentially costly problems such as leaky roofs, cracked tile and uneven framing.

From a December 14, 1991 New York Newsday article, about defective construction in the New York region (italics added):

> Unlike home improvement contractors, home builders are not licensed in New York, as they are in New Jersey and Connecticut. There have been unsuccessful attempts in the state Legislature and in the Suffolk County Legislature to require licensing.
>
> "Our membership has been opposed to it," said [a NY Builders Association official]. "We prefer the point of sale protection rather than the bureaucracy."
>
> That protection is a state-mandated home warranty law that went into effect in 1989. Under the law, buyers have protection against structural defects for six years...The warranty law has been criticized by consumer advocates who say that *a homeowner has little recourse if a builder goes bankrupt or closes the business and incorporates under another name.*

From an article in the Raleigh News and Observer, December 15, 1991:

> In North Carolina, its a simple matter for a contractor who knows he's about to be sued to drain assets from one company and put them in another, according to Bob Garner, a producer/reporter for North Carolina Public Television in Chapel Hill. Garner, who recently produced a documentary on defective residential construction in this state, says that one thing prospective homeowners can do to

protect themselves is check whether their builder has done business under another name.

"Otherwise, you could ask your contractor whether he's had any complaints," Garner said, "and he might respond that ABC Construction Co. has a clean record — we've never had a complaint. He may not tell you that three other companies he had were virtually driven out of business. He just goes and gets a contractors's license under another name."

The bottom line: don't be surprised about builders going bankrupt and starting anew to avoid responsibility. In too many jurisdictions the legal system allows such practice to occur with total impunity.

Between a Rock and a Hard Place

If all this sounds dismal, it is. No homeowner in his right mind wants to go through the nightmare of litigation against a builder: experts invading your home; mountains of paper work; dozens of meetings; enormous legal fees; and time taken away from living and working. There is only one reason any sane homeowner sues his builder: he or she has *NO OTHER CHOICE*. Anyone who thinks otherwise should suffer a defective home built by an uncaring builder.

In the first six months after our nightmare became public, and long before my first book was published, we personally heard from ten local people with construction horror stories of their own. Seven of the ten had already hired lawyers, and had either sued their builder or were about to do so. The other three asked for the name of our attorney. The people who contacted us are just the tip of a large group of oppressed, angry, new-home buyers.

Probably most construction complaints settle without litigation. The builder fixes the problem, or the homeowners accept a substandard repair, or they just give up and make the repairs themselves. None of these options was feasible in our situation. When the builder and architect refused to properly investigate our complaints, we had no rational choice but to call in experts to find out what was wrong. When the experts' reports showed major structural defects we were caught in a legal bind. We could not legally sell the house without disclosure of the reports. With disclosure the house was — for all practical purposes — unsalable. Yet at no time was there any offer by the defendants to fix our house properly.

Over one million new homes are built each year in the United States (two million in boom times). Why don't we hear more about defective construction? Why is this book just about the only one on the subject in print? Defective construction is certainly more common than would appear from a handful of isolated news articles.

Probably many homeowners don't have the resources to sue their builder all the way through trial. Or a lawsuit is not economically feasible. At the very first meeting our litigator remarked that if the defects cost "only $20,000" to fix, a lawsuit might not be worthwhile. As it turned out, our experts said the defects would cost almost $100,000 to properly fix and a lawsuit was still not worthwhile.

But many homeowners do fight back, and the media are just beginning to pay attention. One article on the subject appeared in the Business Section of the November 10, 1991 Los Angeles Times, a paper with a national audience, by reporter Jube Shiver.

Homeowners Are Going After Shoddy Builders

● Complaints about defective construction are on the rise. And more consumers are suing the contractor or even filing fraud charges.

Complaints about housing defects, once mostly confined to builders of low-cost homes in fast-growing suburbs, have spread across the nation in recent months as owners of mid-priced and even luxury houses and condominiums complain of shoddy construction.

Jordan Clark, president of the United Homeowners Assn. in Washington, calls construction defects a "major problem" that has drawn Congress' attention and has sparked homeowner groups from California to Florida to sue inept builders.

In California, until recently the nation's hottest housing market, the state Contractors' License Board says complaints against builders and home repair contractors jumped from 27,500 for the year ended June 30, 1989 to 31,000 in 1991...

...Industry officials say a very small fraction of the 1.1 million homes built each year have significant problems.

Critics say that is because the cost of litigation and the shame of discovering costly defects after living in a house for years prevents most single-family homeowners from suing builders.   What's more, shoddy builders often disband their company and form another one to avoid paying claims on defects — which range from dangerous lapses such as undersized electrical wiring and weak foundations to annoying an potentially costly problems such as leaky roofs, cracked tile and uneven framing.

...Increasingly, homeowners are pooling financial resources to fight shoddy builders. In hearings in September before the House housing subcommittee, more than 300 homeowners in five states came to Washington to complain about serious construction defects in their new homes...

...Among the largest and most active groups is the 1000 member North Carolina Homeowners Assn., formed 2-1/2 years ago because of all the trouble homeowners in the state have had with builders, said Jim Parker, the group's co-founder and president.

Shiver recounts the plight of individual homeowners in North Carolina ("What I went through with that builder was worse than the hell I went through in Vietnam"), Florida ("I was horrified at the condition of the house") and Virginia. A Virginia woman bought a house with a leaky roof, uneven floors, irregular wall studs and an undersized ceiling support beam. Then her builder went out of business.

She found four other homeowners allegedly victimized by the same builder. They joined together and persuaded authorities to arrest the builder on suspicion of criminal fraud. In exchange for dropping the charges, the Fairfax County prosecutor's office got the man to pay [her] $10,000 of the more than $70,000 she and her husband had spent building their house.

The Situation in North Carolina

Several of the news articles quoted so far have been from North Carolina. In recent years there have been more problems there than perhaps in any other state except Florida. In both states the problems are accentuated by much new construction, the result of an influx of retirees and other newcomers.

The situation in North Carolina reflects the nation as a whole, not only the fact of defective construction, but how the victims are affected and how the builders, regulatory agencies and politicians tend to respond. As already pointed out, there are no statistics on defective construction nationwide, or even in any one state. According to a story in the Charlotte Observer from March 17, 1990:

Nobody knows how many people buy new homes with code violations and then can't get their builder to fix them; there is no central system for counting complaints. The Home Builders Association points out that last year 50,000 homes were built in North Carolina, and the state attorney general's office and the contractors' licensing board received about 250 complaints.

But critics of the state's regulatory system say many complaints go unreported because homeowners don't know who to call or they fear they won't be able to sell their house if they complain publicly.

The consumer section of the Attorney General's office estimates that, in general, only 10% of unhappy consumers report complaints. If that were applied to the home building industry, that would

amount to 2,500 complaints in 1989 — one
complaint for every 20 houses built.

That's five percent of new construction in one state. In the
Introduction I estimated the problem at three percent of new
construction nationwide, clearly a conservative estimate.

But statistics are faceless. Three percent, five percent — one
might think it's a small problem. Until you hear from the victims.
From the same Charlotte Observer article (italics added):

> Homeowners who sue builders may win in court
> but because of state law, usually can't collect
> attorney fees. Sometimes homeowners win, but they
> can't collect money from builders shielded by
> bankruptcy laws.
>
> "There are adequate protections through the
> courts and the regulatory board," said...a member of
> the NC Licensing Board for General Contractors.
>
> That's of little comfort to Mrs. P. of Cary, just
> outside Raleigh, who bought her two-story, three-
> bedroom house six years ago for $110,000.
>
> State officials eventually found 10 "plainly visible"
> code violations, including structural problems. A
> jury awarded her $16,500, which she hasn't been
> able to collect from her now-defunct building
> company.
>
> The contractor is not listed in the telephone book
> and couldn't be reached for comment.
>
> "To buy a house is everybody's dreams," said Mrs.
> P., a salesperson for a carpet company. "We had
> worked all our lives for this house. *Then it turned
> into the biggest nightmare anybody could imagine.*"

North Carolina deserves special attention because many
homeowners are beginning to fight for their rights in organized
fashion, through the North Carolina Homeowners Association
(NCHA). The NCHA is a grass roots organization that was
created because of the large amount of defective construction in
that state, and of the perverse way North Carolina's laws have
worked against the homeowner victims. NCHA is dedicated to

both preventing defective construction and to helping victims.

Because of many cases like Mrs. P.'s, the NCHA was instrumental in getting a bill passed in the state legislature to reimburse buyers of defective construction. House Bill 37 provides for reimbursement of repair costs *if* the buyers win a legal judgment *and* the builder goes bankrupt.

One of the problems in North Carolina (and perhaps elsewhere) is that, despite the requirement of a license to be a general contractor, the law is frequently skirted or ignored. Contractors can build houses without a license — and get away with it. In part, this is due to a loophole in the law that allows contractors to build without a license if the house — not counting land and profit — come to less than $45,000. From the Charlotte Observer, March 17, 1990:

> [Homeowner] thought he was dealing with a licensed builder when he signed a contract in 1987 for a $120,000 house on 2.5 acres outside Chapel Hill.
>
> He was wrong.
>
> State investigators later found the house to have structural problems that [homeowner] has spent $7,000 and hundreds of hours to fix.
>
> His builder skirted the law, according to the NC Licensing board for General contractors, by telling local inspectors that construction would cost $25,000.
>
> ...the builder argued that he had not entered into any contracts and did not consider himself a "general contractor."

Earlier I explained why an occupancy permit means nothing about the structural integrity of a new home. In North Carolina the problem has been taken one step further: builders sometimes sell houses *without* a permit. Here are portions of a letter written by a homeowner to the North Carolina Homeowners Association.

> In March of 1990 my husband and I came to Wilmington, NC to build our retirement home...In April of 1990 construction was started. On Nov 1,

1990 [the builder] told us we could move in because all inspections had passed.   According to our contract we were to pay the builder as the house progressed and he in turn would pay all the sub-contractors.

After we moved in there were several items to be completed and after completion we would pay the last 3% balance. We waited until April of 1991 for him to complete the house, but he refused.   It was about that time that we discovered we did not have a certificate of occupancy.   After talking to the county inspectors we discovered that the builder did not comply to certain building codes.   The building inspector said the [the builder] was aware of this and that the certificate of occupancy could not be issued until the violations were corrected.   The inspector again notified [the builder] but he again ignored the request.

We then hired another contractor to correct the violations at our expense in order to receive the certificate of occupancy. We could not understand how a building contractor could refuse to comply to building codes and not even receive a fine.   Nothing was done to this builder.

We still have not had our house completed and we are finding more and more code violations that the county inspector apparently chose to ignore. To top all of this off [the builder] is now suing us for the 3% balance and has put a lien on our house.

After detailing further legal and construction horrors about her house, the homeowner writes:

> We have found that North Carolina
> does not have laws to protect the
> homeowner or they choose not to enforce
> them.

How bad can things get in a new home? Two more examples, from different areas of North Carolina, will show you. In the summer of 1991 Mr. and Mrs. F. contracted to build a new home on five wooded acres in Polk County (western North Carolina, near Spartanburg, SC). According to an April 9, 1992 story in The Tryon Daily Bulletin, within a few months the experience turned into a "a full-fledged nightmare."

While the house was under construction the couple discovered evidence of sloppy construction, and discussed the problems with both their builder and the local building inspector. Some of the problems had to do with the structural integrity of the dwelling, like the placement of foundation piles. At this point the house was about 35% complete. Despite all that the homebuyers saw and documented, the building inspector passed on the construction

> with flying colors. They were shocked and puzzled. How could a trained inspector have overlooked such obvious flaws? they wondered.
>
> ...[They] were not daunted. With the guidance of the North Carolina Homeowners Association, they took steps to resolve their situation. The couple immediately began to document in photos and on video tape everything they felt might be a building code violation in their house.
>
> In addition, the couple asked George Birmingham, a private building consultant with almost 50 years experience as a builder, to evaluate their situation. Birmingham spent hours inspecting the house and his verdict was not good. He enumerated close to 50 problems in his final report including missing or faulty foundation piers and footings, improperly installed shingles, improper truss installation, sloppy masonry and mismatched flue liners.
>
> He concluded his eight page report with the

comment: "I am amazed they got the house built this far without a major collapse or failure with this building." In a telephone interview with *The Bulletin*, he characterized the [couple's] house as "a glaring example of poor workmanship."

In the aggregate, three independent engineering reports showed that the construction

failed to meet the plans and specifications of this custom-designed home [and] failed to even meet minimum N.C. building codes. [The couple] say that the builder refused to take responsibility for problems the studies detailed, claiming instead that there was only one corner of the house out of alignment.

The result? The couple felt they had no choice but to halt construction and sue the builder. At that point they were already out $130,000 — the cost of the land, part of their construction loan, and legal fees. They sued for breach of contract, fraud and deceptive trade practices. The builder then sued *them* for work done on the house but not yet paid for.

Not a happy result when building one's dream home. And exactly who is right and who is wrong? How much damage has been done and who is to pay? Those questions, unfortunately, are now for the courts to decide. I say unfortunate, because anyone reading this article and talking to the couple can only conclude they are innocent victims of incredibly sloppy work. They would not risk losing $130,000 unless absolutely convinced their house was constructed improperly, and that the builder's proposed remedy is inadequate.

Then there is the case of Mr. O., of Cary, NC (a suburb of Raleigh), who bought a new house constructed with 28 building code violations! Eventually his complaints led to suspension of the builder's license for a full year — but not to repair of his house. His case generated many articles in the local newspapers. From the Cary News, November 9, 1991:

[One] member of the Wake [county] homebuilders association who has built homes for 24 years, said the board's decision [to revoke the builder's license] was fair, but far too late for Mr. O.'s sake. I went through his house. "It's probably one of the worst construction jobs I've ever seen. It really is."

Did lifting the builder's license help this homeowner? An editorial on the suspension also appeared in the Cary newspaper.

This week's decision by the N.C. Licensing Board of General Contractors to suspend the license of Cary Builder...was unfortunate because it does nothing to implement changes that appear to be needed in the homebuilding industry.

That there were problems with the house in question has been acknowledged by the builder - that no resolution has occurred also is a fact - and, that the licensing board has too much work and too little time also is evident because the bulk of the case was handled by an administrative law judge at the request of the volunteer board members and their staff.

...As it is, Mr. O.'s house has not been repaired and he says he cannot afford to have it done; [the builder] now has chosen to spend even more money on legal fees to have the case decided by a jury; and, nothing has been resolved.

After reading my first book, Mr. O. wrote me a long letter about his construction nightmare.

Dear Dr. Martin,

I would like to say that I enjoyed reading your book <u>And They Built A Crooked House</u>, but in fact the further along I read the angrier I became. Your book was extremely well written but what angered me was the fact that I could have inserted my name at many places describing the treatment you received upon building your "dream home."

I'm sure you receive many letters from people describing their dream home turned nightmare, so I wouldn't go into great detail about my experiences. I purchased a new 2,800 sq. ft. home in June of 1989 in one of the best developments in North Carolina for $212,000. The builder was held out to be one of the area's finest...

Six months after moving in cracks started developing in the walls of my home. The builder stated "I <u>think</u> there is a pier missing from under this wall." I asked the builder to have a complete structural engineering report done on the home, to which he refused. I then retained my own structural engineer and found (among other things) that:

1. The foundation footings did not comply with the building code.
2. 932 bricks in the foundation were void of mortar in their vertical joints. (The engineer stated that due to the omission of mortar in the joints that the home most probably would collapse in hurricane force winds.)
3. Two load bearing walls were not properly supported.
4. The chimney is not properly supported and is pulling away from the house.

The estimate to repair the foundation alone on this home is $127,000.. The tax assessor did reduce the value [of the home] to $49,000, the cost of the land. I have been denied homeowner's insurance.

After detailing his initial brush with an indifferent legal system in North Carolina, he continues:

> I put $67,000 down on this house and my entire life has become ruined by what has happened with this home. I can only hope that other people will read your book before buying a home...The only way that I could have been aware that this home was defective, prior to purchasing it, was to have dug up the foundation which I eventually did.
>
> I joined a group called the N.C. Homeowners Association. This is a group of homeowners whose lives have been devastated by purchasing defective homes. One member...let his defective home in N.C. go into foreclosure and moved to New York.

What was the builder's response to suspension by the North Carolina licensing board? It is outlined in the following article that also appeared in the Cary, N.C. News (italics added).

> A state licensing board has suspended the license of a Cary building contractor after finding 28 code violations in a $212,000 house in Cary.
>
> "I think it is the least they could have done, considering the shape that my house is in," said Mr. O., noting that [the builder] can continue to build during the appeal. Mr. O. said a defect found in his home was also in other homes that [the builder] built.
>
> [The builder] said that three engineers inspected the home and, although there are code violations in the house, *the building code is not in line with current building practices*...He said that the current 119-page code is ambiguous and that the state will replace it next year with a comprehensive 400-page code.
>
> The board's final decision said that the foundation of the house lacked mortar in vertical

joints, a code violation. Mr. O. said [the builder] testified in a   deposition that "he has built other homes this way and continues to build this way."

Mr. O. said insurance companies refused to issue a policy on the house and real estate agents won't list it for sale.

"Who wants to buy it?" he said.   "It can't be sold."

Viewed from the standpoint of what's right, fair, rational, and proper, this case, like ours and many others, makes no sense to the citizen uninvolved in such matters.   Mr. O.'s house is defective.   Its construction violated state building codes.   The builder disputed these same codes.   He was reprimanded by the Licensing Board.   The house was unsalable.   The builder would not fix it, leaving the homeowner no choice but to fight an expensive and enervating legal battle.   Yet the legal system is woefully unable to effect any equitable solution (as Mr. O. makes abundantly clear in other correspondence).

In the world of defective construction what's right, fair and rational is usually of no consequence.   In the real world of defective construction, homeowners are caught in a Kafkaesque situation; the bad builders are often rewarded (with profits), and the homeowners are invariably victimized (with legal expenses and loss of property value).   This is the real world in North Carolina and everywhere else.

We chose to fight our case all the way to trial instead of give up and, like Mr. O., met up against people who make their own rules, rewrite history, delay, deny, distort.   Mr. O. went further, and met even more resistance than we did.   Mr. O. generated so much heat about his case that the town of Cary, NC actually referred to him at one point as a "loose cannon" because, he says, "I decided to fight back rather than go into a corner and die." (Mr. O.'s case against the builder eventually settled out of court for an undisclosed sum.)

The North Carolina Homeowners Association publishes a newsletter (see Appendix for address).   A recent edition quoted me in the lead paragraph.

North Carolina Homeowners Association
- - - - - -
Words can't express what we have been going through. The total frustration coupled with a sense of moral outrage. The sense of loss. The feelings of helplessness. It is the material equivalent of rape. This is how wars start. In a less civilized world...there would be physical violence over this. These irresponsible men have disfigured our home, our lives, our sensibilities.
— Dr. Ruth S. Martin
And They Built A Crooked House (1991)

Outrage and Frustration
These powerful words express the despair of a homeowner victimized by fraud, deception, and irresponsibility in the construction of her "dream" home. I need your help to expose and correct serious problems in the residential construction industry in North Carolina. Hundreds of innocent families have been financially and emotionally devastated by the purchase of defective new houses. Without changes, thousands more will suffer a similar fate.

North Carolina's elected representatives passed laws requiring licensing of contractors and establishing minimum safety standards for home construction. THESE LAWS ARE NOT ENFORCED! Local building inspections departments and state regulatory boards ignore serious violations of the building code, first by approving defective houses and then by doing nothing when homeowners are stuck with the results.

Homeowners with defective homes are surprised that they are not protected...

This and other editions of the NCHA newsletter have documented the weaknesses of North Carolina laws, their lack of enforcement, the outright fraud found in many situations, and how the Homeowner's Recovery Fund passed in the state legislature over the fierce opposition of home builders. Because of NCHA's efforts, the specific problems in North Carolina and the reasons behind them are perhaps better documented than in any other state.

Dr. Donald Jacob is one of the strongest voices in the NCHA, although he now lives in New York. Dr. Jacob bought a defective home in North Carolina in 1986, and within two years discovered that the foundation was totally substandard. In his long (and futile) attempt to get the house repaired, he discovered much evidence of fraud and deceit, not just in the erection of his house but in many others.   Working with the NCHA, he uncovered and documented the following circumstances in North Carolina.

- Homes in North Carolina have been approved by local building inspectors despite serious, flagrant Building Code violations. Some licensed building inspectors, engineers and architects are providing North Carolina contractors with documents falsely certifying compliance with the State Building Code. Builders use these documents to deceive unsuspecting homebuyers.

- The North Carolina courts are lenient in allowing builders to declare bankruptcy and avoid compensating damaged homeowners if they win an award from a jury.

- The North Carolina construction boom started in the early 1980s. Contractors licenses were handed out not just to builders, but to politicians, salesmen, real estate agents and any local businessmen with access to capital. More dependent upon financial status than knowledge of construction principles, the licensing process did nothing to protect citizens from incompetent contractors.

- The North Carolina Contractors Licensing Board is funded entirely by fees collected from contractors. Five of the 7 members are contractors. The Board has consistently refused to enforce North Carolina laws related to construction.

- The North Carolina civil courts have exhibited a peculiar inability to compensate homebuyers damaged by negligent or dishonest construction. Through a technique called corporation folding, North Carolina contractors can change the name of their company every few years and drain all assets from the old company. The courts have refused to use the personal assets of negligent contractors for compensation. Therefore, even if he wins in court, the homeowner can collect no money.

So this is North Carolina, where outraged homeowners are more organized than in any other state. But problems with defective construction — and the homeowner's no-win position — exist all over the country. Why can't people who buy a seriously defective new house get it fixed?

Why Can't Americans Get Their New House Fixed?

The typical response of builders and developers to this litany of horror stories is something like the following: 'Sure, there are some bad builders out there. But there are bad doctors, too. And bad lawyers, accountants, and car salesmen. Most people who buy a new house are very happy with their home. The incidence of truly bad construction is very small. You are blowing this thing out of all proportion.'

That is the argument. And it completely misses the point. It is a defense against an attack which does not exist. My recitation of these horror stories is not an attack on the construction industry or on home builders in general. I am not trying to reform an industry that is comprised of over 100,000 individual contractors, and whose bad apple builders are scattered among thousands of jurisdictions. My task is far more focused: to help the individual homebuyer protect himself or herself against man-made mistakes and a hostile and unhelpful legal system. For me to argue against the self-serving propaganda of builders and developers would be a futile effort, of no help to anyone.

I have no doubt that the vast majority of builders are both competent and honest. That fact does not help the small but significant number of homeowners who are devastated by bad construction. And devastation is an appropriate term. It is unconscionable for anyone who buys a fully-guaranteed new home to have to go to court because the house was not constructed according to local building codes. It is unconscionable for anyone to lose a fortune because the law allows a builder to sell a defective house, declare bankruptcy and then continue building houses under a new name. It is unconscionable for anyone to be sold a new house that should never have passed inspection.

Lawyers have a term for the situation as it exists with defective construction: *res ipsa loquitur*, the thing speaks for itself. The fact is, there are thousands of unhappy homebuyers, victims of defective construction. They can be found in every state of the union. The fact is, our system of litigation and laws is not designed to help the victims achieve meaningful redress. If anything, the legal system penalizes the buyer of a defective house because of the enormous cost to litigate and the irrevocable loss of those funds. The fact is, there is no real penalty for dishonest and unethical builders, developers and home inspectors. The fact is, the laws in every state are powerless to make a builder comply with existing building codes, to make a builder fix his mistakes, or even to make a builder pay a legal judgment.

All this is true, but the most crucial fact is that, for the individual homebuyer, the risk of acquiring a structurally defective home can be significantly reduced by taking a few very important steps. After all, the problems occur in something completely man-made. We are not talking about the variables of human disease, or acts of God, or the whims of a judge or jury. There is no way for any given client to always check if his or her doctor or lawyer is doing the right thing. There *is* a way for every homebuyer to help ensure that his house is being, or has been, constructed properly.

The majority of construction nightmares around the country do not result from outright, intentional fraud (a situation more often found in the home repair business). Fraud in constructing and inspecting new houses does exist, as has been documented in North Carolina and elsewhere, but by and large contractors building a house want and expect things to go right; most cases of defective construction don't start out with a builder intending to cheat the homebuyer.

Defective construction happens, unfortunately, because many builders just don't know how to build a good house or care about the result. They are not only bad builders in the hands-on sense, but also bad managers of craftsmen and subcontractors. No matter how well intentioned they may have been before the project began, the finished house reflects sloppy, careless, and incompetent work.

When a bad builder's construction errors are exposed he is apt to display the traits of bad people: dishonesty, denial, distortion of the truth, outright lying, vindictiveness. He does not accept responsibility and may actually fight the complainers. As a result, the homeowners are left hanging; the more they document the defects, the more likely the builder will ignore the problems.

Homeowners saddled with a seriously defective house often dig a hole for themselves, albeit unwittingly. They thoroughly document the problems yet cannot get them fixed by the people who caused them, and their documentation makes the house unsalable. In desperation, the homeowners call upon the legal system; they hire a lawyer. Unfortunately, from that point the situation almost invariably goes from bad to worse, as the builder also hires a lawyer. Lawyers hired by builders are trained to fight first and settle later. Or fight forever and settle never. Lawyers for builders know that the legal system is on the side of the builders and against the homeowners, and they take every advantage of this fact.

*   *   *

When spokesmen for the building or real estate industries say that "a very small fraction of the 1.1 million homes built each year have significant problems," what does that mean? Three percent is a "very small fraction," but that represents over 30,000 homebuying families! And if it's 5,000 or 80,000 defective houses each year, so what? The problem only has to happen to you *once*.

Behind every story I have quoted — and these stories are but a tiny sample of the construction nightmares documented year after year — is a family full of heartache, disappointment, crumbling dreams. Buy a defective house from an irresponsible builder and you buy a nightmare beyond belief.

The solution as I see it is not to "fix" the industry, for that is impossible, given the huge diversity among both builders and the jurisdictions where they do business. All the housing regulation in the past 50 years has done nothing for buyers of defective houses. The solution — the only realistic solution — is for you, the consumer of new construction, to become smarter, wiser, tougher.

SECTION 3. Why do the bad guys win? A psychiatrist looks for some answers

> The only thing necessary for the triumph of evil is for good men to do nothing.
> — Edmund Burke (1729-1797)

Every profession has its bad apples. Law, medicine, architecture, accounting, real estate — they all contain members who are an embarrassment to the vast majority of honest, ethical practitioners. In analyzing the myriad reports of victimized home owners, I am struck by how often the underlying, root cause in most horror stories seems to be 'bad people'. I don't mean the honest builder who makes a mistake. We all make mistakes. I mean those people who are dishonest, mean spirited, deceptive, deceitful; people who make mistakes and lie about them. People like our developer, Jake Cooper.

These people would rather spend money on lawyers to fight you instead of investigating your complaint or fixing the problem. They seem completely unconcerned about their reputation or your satisfaction. These are people who, because of deep seated psychological flaws, seek to hurt customers who complain instead of trying to help them. I believe that 'bad people' are responsible for much of the heartache and emotional trauma suffered by victims of defective construction.

Why do bad people get away with hurting others so easily, with causing so much trouble? The problem, of course, is not confined to the housing industry. Many best selling books have recounted the greed and dishonesty of people in the business world, of how they get away with their unethical behavior, and of the lawyers who help them succeed. Read these books for a flavor of what you are up against when the people selling you a product prove dishonest, or when they hire lawyers to fight a legitimate complaint. Several books of this genre are listed in the Bibliography.

These books cover such topics as the savings & loan scandal, Wall Street buyouts, stockbroker dishonesty and bank fraud. They are about complex dealings that involve lawyers, bankers, accountants, real estate executives, politicians and, above all, innocent people getting hurt. Some people see these stories as exemplifying the Greed of the 1980s. Others find in them signs of the decay of civilization. Still others see nothing more significant than a few bad guys getting caught with their hands in a gigantic cookie jar. Different people will no doubt come away with varying perspectives after reading these books.

Here's what I glean from the stories told in these books. Except for the most egregious of the players, like Dennis Levine, Michael Milken, Ivan Boesky, Charles Keating, and Robert Maxwell, most businessmen get away unscathed with unethical behavior that lines their pockets at the expense of innocent victims. Read these books and you will see that only a tiny percentage of the bad guys ever get caught or punished or penalized financially. The vast majority of unethical dealers get away completely with their chicanery. And the victims? Most of them never recoup anything more than a fraction of their losses. Billions lost to the S&L failures. Billions lost to BCCI. Billions lost to Drexal Burnham. And where do these billions of dollars come from? From thousands upon thousands of innocent people.

Of course, defective construction is seldom the result of conspiracy or fraud in the legal definition. People become victims when bad guys screw up and refuse to follow through, honor a guarantee, or make good on their work. Instead of outright, provable fraud, the root causes are much more mundane: incompetency, greed, inability to admit a mistake, lying, mean-spiritedness — traits that are often displayed by 'bad people'.

Our architect and builder were incompetent by anyone's standard, and could not admit their mistakes. Our developer was greedy and provably dishonest. The defendants' lawyers did nothing meaningful to resolve the dispute or investigate our complaints. At no time was a realistic and honest offer made to fix our house, or satisfy our complaint. In any major dispute over defective construction, when the root cause is bad people, you will find a similar set of players, and similar consequences for the homeowners.

*   *   *

The arch villain in our case was the developer Jake Cooper, who profited by his unethical behavior. In philosophy, if not in style and methods, he is like other unethical businessmen whose actions are chronicled in the modern best sellers. The message to Cooper and other businessmen of no integrity is apparent: if you can profit by misrepresenting a guarantee or reneging on a contract, your chances of penalty are almost zero. That's the message I read in these books and in our trial judge's decision. It is a sad, sad message for America.

Our developer's 'quick-profit-no-responsibility' plan was stalled by our lawsuit, but not for long. He didn't make the quick second profit no doubt expected when he bought the house back, but I am confident he didn't lose money either (especially considering his $50,000 profit the first time around). Nor, I feel certain, did he lose any sleep in the three years between our first letter asking for his help (December 1986) and the time he re-sold the house (March 1990).

This experience was a true mid-life crisis for me and my family. To Jake Cooper the litigation was only a minor annoyance, like a mosquito at a picnic that you finally brush away. Unhappy homeowners, angry letters, lawsuit, depositions, a trial — all are part of doing business as a builder and developer. No big deal.

Businessmen like Jake Cooper hurt others and feel no pain while doing so. They can make money by deceiving people or reneging on contracts, careful to avoid breaking any specific laws. If they have to go to court for breach of contract, that is only a civil (as opposed to criminal) matter, and just part of the routine of doing business.

You can get five years in the slammer for stealing a loaf of bread from the neighborhood supermarket, but if you "steal" a thousand loaves of bread by reneging on your contract there is no penalty. It is not 'against' any law to breach a contract, or to deceive homebuyers with promises you don't intend to keep. The same is true, of course, with virtually all types of consumer misrepresentation. A dishwasher and a house are treated the same in the eyes of the law.

So while it may be unethical, immoral, or abhorrent to sell a defective house and renege on all promises and written guarantees, it is not illegal. (In virtually all jurisdictions you have to prove outright fraud — *intent* to deceive — to have an illegal situation. The judge in our case did not accept that Cooper intended to defraud us, despite his lying and malicious behavior before the trial, and his total denial of all responsibility.) Because it is not illegal to breach a contract, even with malice, Cooper was able to convince himself and his cronies that they had done nothing wrong, as if deceiving others and lying is what decent people do all the time.

Why do the bad guys win? The answer is simple. If they can make a buck by hurting someone, and their actions do not clearly and unequivocally violate criminal law, they will get away with it. They know that no one will stop them. Our society is so burdened by examples of unlawful, unethical, immoral and deceitful behavior, on so many levels, that absent a criminal prosecution, perpetrators of such behavior have nothing to fear. Not civil litigation, not government regulations, not peer disapproval, not social ostracism.

Good people — you, me, and the vast majority of Americans who do not profit by lying and deceiving — are daily bombarded by stories of greedy politicians, businessmen, lawyers, and others. We shake our heads, wish it weren't so, and hope "someone" will do something about it. With rare exception, no one ever does. And that is why, also with rare exception, bad people come to be rewarded by their bad actions. They are free of the psychological barriers that keep good people from lying, cheating, reneging, deceiving. And they do not worry about retribution, because there will be none. They have learned to profit by behavior that would turn the stomach of most decent, honest citizens.

*   *   *

As a psychiatrist I can perhaps explain something about the psychology of bad people like our developer, what makes them 'tick'. This information may help you avoid the pain we endured. Although we didn't realize what we were up against until it was too late, you may find earlier clues in the people you deal with.

In my professional opinion, Cooper's behavior in our case is typical of people who inflict pain on others without feeling pain themselves. Chances are you have run into this type, known in psychiatric jargon as the sociopath or "antisocial personality disorder." A personality disorder is a pathological (not normal) 'equilibrium state' in which the individual displays both occupational and interpersonal dysfunction. The antisocial personality maintains his (or her) state of equilibrium by inflicting pain on others, and *feels no pain while doing so*. The most extreme examples are serial murderers, rapists, and chronic child or spouse abusers.

The disorder can manifest in less extreme ways. The vast majority of these "bad people" — people who hurt others without feeling pain — are certainly not murderers or rapists or criminals in any sense of the word; instead, they have what psychiatrists call an *antisocial character trait*, a *tendency* toward antisocial or deviant behavior that arises in certain situations.

For example, we heard nothing about Cooper's lack of business integrity before our dealings with him. His antisocial trait became apparent when he was faced with the choice of acting responsibly (and risking the loss of money) or acting irresponsibly and inflicting pain on others (us). He utilized the coping mechanism of flagrant externalization (he lied and blamed us) when he was proven to have breached his contract and was publicly exposed.

The equilibrium of people with the antisocial personality trait is maintained by taking advantage of others, hurting people needlessly, telling obvious lies, being physically or verbally abusive, etc. Such behavior helps these bad people to maintain their psychologic equilibrium. Only their victims feel pain.

People with the antisocial personality trait lack "conscience," or what psychiatrists call the superego. In psychiatric jargon, these people have "holes" in their superego. If you end up in an argument with such a person it is best to understand early on what you are up against. You can't fight these people, except in a narrow legal sense, *because they feel no pain or guilt* for their dishonest behavior.

The thing that matters the least to this type of person is *you*, your feelings, your sense of injustice. Don't waste time hoping he will change behavior or attitude because of *your* pain, suffering and anguish. He won't. Finally, don't rely on his good will or sense of decency to do the right thing. If you have been hurt by someone with antisocial tendencies, understand that he (or she) is beyond feeling any pain, remorse, or guilt for what he did to you. If you try to reason with him or appeal to any sense of decency or ask for succor you will just be hurt further. That is a path to total frustration and self defeat.

What are signs of people with antisocial personality tendencies? Here are some strong indicators:

- They don't return your phone calls or answer letters, even when they have a moral or ethical obligation to do so.

- They make no attempt to reason with you, explain their actions, or negotiate honestly.

- They lie about you to others. Not white lies, but blatant, provable lies, often blaming you for a problem *they* created.

- They don't care what you say or to whom you say it (unless what you say costs them money). Their behavior is unchangeable by anything you say or do.

- When recounting events concerning a dispute (e.g., in courtroom testimony, press interviews, or conversations with mutual acquaintances) they present convincing revisionist history; the story they tell is apt to be a "believable" but gross distortion of the truth, designed to suit their purpose and maintain psychological equilibrium.

*   *   *

Integrity can be defined as doing the right or decent thing when you are not compelled by any law or social pressure. Cooper's sociopathic behavior translated into a lack of integrity in our case, and that was our undoing. Certainly a developer with any integrity would have acted differently, would have come in, examined the house, talked to us, helped mediate a settlement, explained his position, *sought a resolution*. Cooper did nothing despite his solicitation of our business, his verbal promises, a written contract, and a handsome profit he made on the deal.

I've explained why a bad person like Jake Cooper behaves in such a manner. But how did it come about that he profited by such behavior? How can this happen in America, that innocent people buying a new house lose money while the guilty party profits?

Do we blame our contract lawyer? Sure, for without a doubt his contract was worthless to our purpose. Do we blame our litigator? Certainly our plight was not his fault, and he did work very hard on the case. But was the abysmal outcome the result of bad legal advice? We'll never know, of course, but his strategy did somehow lead us into a no-win, money-losing legal situation. We are still not sure what strategy might have provided a fairer outcome.

Perhaps our litigator should have come to realize before the trial that the Judge was not sympathetic to our plight, because of numerous pre-trial hearings that went nowhere, and insisted on a jury. Or perhaps he should have pursued Cooper for malicious breach of contract or fraudulent misrepresentation, and not expended his efforts (and our money) against Cooper's incompetent cronies. Or perhaps he should have had us plead for the costs of repair and damages, instead of recision of the contract. Who knows if a different courtroom personality, or a different legal strategy, would have lead to a fairer outcome?

Do we blame ourselves? Yes, but only for being so trusting, and for not being more careful in choosing our builder, architect and contract lawyer. The plain truth, though, is that we were probably more deliberative than nine out of ten people who build a new house. It is just that we needed to be ten out of ten when up against someone like Jake Cooper.

Early on in this case Cooper realized that he could profit by lying and reneging. The ineffectiveness of our lawyers — contract and trial — and a compliant legal system first made his behavior possible, then made it profitable. We had never done business with such a blatantly dishonest businessman, but that is probably because we don't do much business, at least not the type that involves contracts and large sums of money.

Business people tell us that the Jake Coopers of the world are a dime a dozen, that reneging on contracts happens all the time in business transactions. In the business world, they say, you come to expect this sort of thing from a certain percentage of people. One must assume, of course, that there are plenty of sociopaths in the business world. Viewed simply as a business deal, perhaps what happened to us is not all that unusual.

What made it so painful for us is that this was our home, one we had nurtured from the ground up. The defects were not in some office building or warehouse, but in the place where we live and raise our three children. Our emotional attachment to this particular 'business deal' was completely lost on the men who desecrated our home, and on their lawyers.

We always knew in a general way that this was a business deal (hadn't we gone to a contract lawyer to be protected?), but never seriously considered that someone would openly and brazenly breach his contract for further profit *and get away with it*. But it happens. Perhaps our story will sensitize you to two sobering facts:

1)   **That new house you buy is your home, but just another business deal for someone else.**

2)   **There are plenty of bad people in the business world.**

Section 4. How to prevent a nightmare from developing with *your* new home

> Yet the dream of building one's custom home goes on. It should go on. You should know that when you bring together sound information and knowledge, the risks can be managed and your custom dream home can become a reality.
>
> — Charles J. Daniels, *Dream House, Real House. The Adventure of Planning and Building a Custom House*, Macmillan Publishing Co., 1989.

By taking a few deliberate steps you can safeguard the integrity and value of your new house or condominium. The emotional, legal, and financial nightmare many new-home buyers experience *can* be prevented.

Be forewarned. You will likely meet resistance as you try to protect yourself. Your builder, architect, developer, real estate agent — anyone you depend on — may protest as you try to protect yourself legally and financially. They may say you are too cautious, too suspicious, not trusting enough, or they may fall back on their 'reputation' for honesty and integrity. If so, run the other way. It is your home that needs protection, not theirs.

The builder, especially, may even refuse to do business with you. If so, count yourself lucky. Don't make the mistake of assuming there is only one lot, one location, one opportunity for you. Your friends may say you're foolish, that Builder X constructs solid houses with no major problems. But remember: past performance is no guarantee of future quality. In truth, most builders merely subcontract out their work, often to the lowest bidders. If the builder refuses to make himself financially and legally responsible for the construction of your home, go elsewhere. Unless you protect yourself ahead of time *YOU CAN ONLY LOSE IF YOUR HOUSE IS BUILT DEFECTIVELY.*

You must act to protect yourself against major construction

and design mistakes. Furthermore, you must ensure that defects will be fixed if, despite all your precautions, they do show up. In this chapter I will make some definite recommendations on how to protect yourself. (Some of these recommendations, such as thorough house inspection by an independent inspector and engineer, and a healthy wariness toward real estate agents, apply equally well to purchasing a used home.)

*   *   *

First, let me answer a question that might concern some readers: Who am I to make these recommendations? I am not a lawyer, builder, architect, engineer, accountant, real estate agent, or developer. I am not even a businesswoman. By profession I am a psychiatrist, and this book was written in my spare time. How can a full time psychiatrist possibly have the expertise to advise you, the potential home buyer? I have three responses to this most legitimate question.

1) I've been there. Unless people have experienced the agony of defective construction, the futility of litigation against irresponsible business people, they are unlikely to realize how bad things can get when buying a new house (or, for that matter, a used one).

2) I have dealt with numerous other victims, read their stories, talked to them on the phone. And I have treated several of them professionally, for depression and anxiety arising from a defective house. I've seen couples on the brink of divorce, grown men cry in my office, people openly contemplate suicide because the house of their dreams has turned into an unrelieved nightmare.

And I've learned that the consequences of defective construction are the same everywhere. When people buy a defective house and can't get it fixed, the scenario is strikingly similar. (This scenario assumes the builder has not skipped town, something that has happened to many unlucky homebuyers.) Typically, the builder first denies that construction problems in your house exist (our obviously sloping floors were called an "optical illusion"). As the homeowners continue to complain, the builder, instead of dealing forthrightly with the problems, begins to externalize and blame others: "I only do what my architect tells me." "It's not my fault but the fault of the plumber/electrician/ mason/roofer."

When the mistakes are not corrected the builder finally blames the homeowner, criticizing her [usually her] for "blowing the problems out of all proportion," a phrase much favored by builders caught in their mistakes. Or: "She's very picky. Nothing pleases her." This kind of defensive posturing — first denial, then blaming other workmen, then blaming the homeowner — protects the builder from feeling any guilt or discomfort about his mistakes.

Finally, the homeowners hire a lawyer because they have no other rational choice. At this point the builder also goes to his attorney, convinced the homeowners are being unreasonable. From there, it is (sadly) downhill, as the builder's attorney throws up roadblocks to any resolution. The homeowners suffer delays, denials and, all too often, calumny. They are apt to be vilified in legal-sounding letters (as we were). Instead of properly investigating the complaints and working to achieve a resolution, the builder spends money to *fight* the homeowners. (Not infrequently, once the homeowners file a lawsuit the builder will countersue, in order to intimidate them.)

The emotional consequences of this scenario are predictable for the homeowners: depression, anger, despair, a sense of loss. In my first book I described this experience as "the material equivalent of rape." That has turned out to be a most appropriate description.

The fact that this experience is so similar everywhere means there are basic steps anyone can take to protect their investment and avoid the horrors of a legal fight. The universality of this experience also answers another frequently-asked question: Aren't every state's laws different, and doesn't that make advice in one state invalid in another?

Well, I am not a lawyer but I do know this: states may have different statutes about house construction and contracts and builder's warranties, but the result is the same all over. The buyer of defective construction is, in practical and financial terms, unprotected by the law if the builder reneges. There is no state law that protects the home buyer without that person first expending an enormous sum for legal and experts fees, money which cannot be recovered. Indeed, *no matter what contracts have been signed*, there is no law in the land designed to fairly compensate the purchaser of defective residential construction.

3) All the professionals involved in selling real estate (new or used) have a vested interest *different from yours*. The real estate agent, builder, developer, banker and architect all want to sell houses, not warn you of how to prevent defects and litigation. They want you to be happy with your purchase, of course, but rarely will they advise how to protect yourself in the event of problems. Why? Because *they don't want to admit that problems might occur.*

The professionals know that, after you take title to the house or condo, they have your money and are practically immune from your complaints. Yes, immune. After title transfers you have given up all leverage to make anyone follow through on promises or guarantees. From that point onward, you cannot achieve redress without also inflicting great harm on yourself and expending thousands of dollars.

To properly warn is to needlessly scare away potential customers. The people in a position to profit only have to sell you that new house or condominium *once*. They don't care about your repeat business because you are not expected to ever buy another new house, at least not from the same people. That is one reason why you'll find no information from the building or real estate industry about the risks inherent in buying a new house, and why you will almost never hear a real estate agent or builder or developer advising you to hire an independent inspector before purchasing new construction.

To professionals on the selling end, nothing can go wrong, nothing should go wrong, and you have nothing to worry about. They will advise you to insure against fire and theft and earthquake and perhaps even flood in some areas, but never against manmade disaster — faulty design and construction.

When things go right these professionals are some of the nicest people you'll ever meet. But if things go wrong in a major way, you are apt to encounter a "drop dead" attitude from the same people who were all smiles when they took your money. You only have to experience this once to see what I mean.

So a psychiatrist who only wanted a decently-constructed house in which to live and raise her family has, by default, become an advisor on how to protect your investment in a new home. Professionals in law, architecture, construction, and real estate might be amused by my avocation, but just remember this: My husband and I (as have countless others) hired a professional contract lawyer to help protect our investment. We (and countless others) had a professional, licensed builder construct our house. We (and countless others) used the services of a licensed architect. We (and countless others) had faith that professionals would know how to design, build, and contractually guarantee for us a well-built house. But in the end the work of these professionals was so very, very bad, that in fact it was *un*professional. As a result we (as have countless others) lost a lot of money and incurred a lot of aggravation. Don't let this happen to you. It is caveat emptor all the way.

* * *

1. CHECK OUT EVERYONE: BUILDER, DEVELOPER, ARCHITECT.

You're not buying a piece of land and a house; you're buying a builder. More to the point, you're buying a builder's reputation.
— *Joys and Perils of That Unbuilt House.* Changing Times Magazine, June 1990, pages 41-49.

Very often you will be dealing with local individuals who only build in your area. In fact, the higher priced the house the more likely the builder is self employed and not working for a large firm. Whether your house is constructed by such local people or by a national firm means nothing in terms of quality. You need to thoroughly check out the people you are dealing with in any situation.

There were three defendants in our case, all self-employed. The architect and builder were shown to be incompetent in the design and construction of our house, respectively. All three men lacked integrity, but the architect and developer were particularly bad; they lied to newspaper reporters to in an attempt to resell the defective house.

In the very beginning, of course, we started out cautiously, making what we thought were all the right moves. We had no inkling whatsoever of the trap we were entering. Just how did two hard working professionals get hooked up with three no-good people in the construction of their $350,000 dream house? Easy. *We were not careful enough.*

We wanted a particular lot so we took what came with it: the developer owner, and his architect and builder. We did not investigate these people except in the most cursory way. We assumed the developer was honest simply because a) he was rich and lived in a high class suburb nearby, b) we were moving next door to his son, and c) his grandchildren and our kids were in the same schools. We actually thought this set of circumstances conferred some type of protection on our deal. Why, we figured, would this nice rich man want to cheat *us*?

We also assumed the builder and architect were competent, mainly because they were building the house next door, for the developer's son. My husband and I talked about the circumstances, analyzed them repeatedly, and just *assumed* everything would be OK. Given the same set of circumstances, you might have reached the same conclusions.

Well, we were fooled. You cannot assume anything in an area as important as building or buying your new home. Inspect — not just look at — other homes your builder, developer or architect have built or designed. Demand references. Dig for information, then check it out. Call people. We didn't check out these men, demand references, or even talk to other business contacts. Such investigation might still not have uncovered their incompetency, or the developer's flagrant dishonesty in our deal, but we didn't think *to ask*. Like countless other naive home buyers with busy schedules, we assumed, for what turned out to be all the wrong reasons, that we were dealing with competent and fair-minded people.

How do you do it? How do you check out builders, architects, developers? Some advisors recommend you call the Better Business Bureau to inquire about a particular builder or developer. This is a common sense first step but not apt to be all that helpful, for several reasons: 1) builders construct houses under many different names; Joe Blow may have several complaints registered under ABC Construction but none under XYZ Homebuilders, the company you are contracting with; 2) serious complaints usually don't go to the BBB (ours didn't), but instead to a lawyer or arbitrator; 3) the form required to file a complaint is long and cumbersome, and many people just don't bother registering their complaints; 4) the BBB is a business-supported organization, not a consumer-supported one. Its primary goal is to protect legitimate businessmen from the fallout of bad businessmen, not to protect the consumer. While one hopes that the BBB's primary goal meshes with consumer protection, keep in mind that the BBB was set up to protect businesses, not consumers. In short, don't rely on any business-supported agency when checking out your builder. You need to be your own sleuth.

After it became apparent that our house was defective, the builder, when asked by potential clients about his other houses, did not disclose that he had built any homes on our street (he built three, all defective to some degree; ours was by far the worst). A prudent homebuyer who learned what he built for us would think twice before doing business with him.

I recommend you ask your prospective builder for the names of people who have bought his *last five houses*. Repeatedly emphasize that you want his last five. Not his best five, his first five, or five good ones, but the *last five*. Tell him all you want are the names, and the phone numbers or addresses. If he balks, or says he doesn't remember, or makes some other flimsy excuse, walk. If he refuses on the grounds he doesn't want to invade the privacy of his customers, be skeptical.   Good builders give references all the time.   If he gives you the addresses but no phone numbers, you can easily get the phone numbers from the city directory.   If the phone number is unlisted, go to the door during daylight hours and knock.   Or, write a letter to the homeowner, giving your phone number and asking the person to please call you.

People who bought a house from the builder will level with you, good or bad. If you hear five good recommendations, you've likely found a good builder.   If you encounter any seriously disgruntled homeowner, try to get the complete story about what happened.   If you are satisfied the builder acted properly there may be no cause for alarm.   But what if you discover that two of the last five home buyers are suing the builder!   Won't you be happy you called?   Whatever you find, if there is doubt don't proceed.   It's not worth it.

One last recommendation.   On principle, don't use a friend or relative to build your house.   Any non-business relationship you have with the builder will compromise your alternatives if things go wrong.

2.   **CHECK OUT THE COMPANY**.   What goes for the individual, self-employed builder goes for the large company as well.   Many houses in the mid- and lower-price ranges are built by large regional or national construction companies. These firms can't possibly construct every house with uniform high quality, especially since they are dependent on the vagaries of local workmen.   Don't get caught with the worst of their output.

On the next page is a table listing eight publicly traded home-building companies.   Note that even the largest companies are tiny compared to the auto giants, and you are probably unfamiliar with them.   The largest U.S. builder of single family homes is Centex Corporation, which trades on the New York Stock Exchange (CTX).

The number of homes sold by Centex in 1990, 7862, represents less than half of one percent of all the new homes sold that year. All seven companies together built less than two percent of the 1,100,000 new homes sold in 1990.

Publicly traded home building companies (ranked by revenues)
(Source: Value Line; NA = not available)

Company	No. Homes Built in U.S. (1991)	No. Employees	1991 Revenues ($billion)	Most Active States or Areas
Centex Corp.	7862	4200	2.16	Sunbelt + midwest
Kaufman & Broad Home Corp.	4456	1000	1.22	CA
PHM Corp. (Pulte Home Corp.)	6686	1500	1.21	13 states
Ryland Group	NA	2452	.86	13 states
Hovnanian Enterprises	2383	550	.30	NJ, FL, PA, NC
Lennar Corp.	NA	1017	.26	AZ, FL, TX
Standard Pacific	NA	553	.26	CA
Toll Brothers	676	438	.18	NJ, PA, DE

Contrast these companies with General Motors, which sold 2,470,000 cars in the U.S. in 1991, or approximately 28% of the U.S. market, and had 1991 worldwide revenues of *$123 billion dollars*. GM can afford to back up its cars with uniform guarantees. Do the large home builders, woefully tiny by comparison, back up their houses, and if so, exactly how? You need to find out.

In the recent recession many large companies actually went under, including U.S. Home, the country's eighth largest home builder at the time it filed for bankruptcy in April 1991. If you buy a home from a large company that goes bankrupt, you have little chance of collecting on any claim. You become, in effect, another creditor. This, of course, is equally true with small local companies, which are much more likely to file for bankruptcy than a large corporation. In either case you are out of luck. That is one more reason why you should not assume you are fully protected by the builder's guarantee.

What if you know a company is financially healthy? That information may be helpful if you are investing in the company, but is of little value if you are buying one of its houses. Ignore the value of the company's stock, corporate reports, or glowing accounts from salesmen when making your decision to buy a house. Such information means nothing about *your* house's quality. The company may be solid in its balance sheet but weak in building houses in your area, on your street. As with the self-employed builder, you cannot assume that a large company built your house well, or that the company will be responsive if there is a major screw up.

Elsewhere in this book are articles about lawsuits against some of the major publicly-held companies. All large companies have been sued by homeowners at one time or other. Because these large companies build so many houses, and lawsuits against them sometimes involve many homeowners in one subdivision, you are more apt to read about them in the newspaper than when a single family sues over one house.

Publicity about lawsuits against these large companies should not scare you away; it merely demonstrates that you have to be careful no matter who you buy your house from, a corporate giant or Joe the local builder. No data exist on the subject, but it is possible that the large companies have a *better* track record in building quality homes than do the small, local builders.

Ask the salesman for names of people in your area who have recently bought houses from the company. This information may be harder to obtain than from a strictly local builder. If possible, though, look at other houses built by the same corporation *in which people are currently living*. Equally important, talk to the occupants. You want to know about any complaints and, in particular, how the company responded to those complaints. If all you hear are positive word-of-mouth recommendations from other home buyers, that is reassuring, but it doesn't guarantee *your* house's integrity, especially if the previous buyers are in another community. Your new house may be constructed by people newly hired by the company. Or it may be in a new subdivision built on improperly-drained swamp land. Or the local house inspector may be just a little too lax for this particular project. Check things out! Assume nothing. (If the house is already built, at least follow the advice in Recommendation 8.)

3. MAKE SURE "THEY" ARE INSURED. "They" is anyone signing your contract, or who could conceivably be sued for problems relating to your new home. Insurance should cover defects found *after* you move in. Many builders and architects are not insured. Architects as professionals can buy malpractice insurance similar in nature to what most doctors carry. Our architect, in casual conversation when we began the design process, told us he was insured. Two years later, when sued, he had no insurance. He either lied or dropped his policy soon after we talked with him.

Our builder was insured, but we believe the architect's lack of insurance proved a major stumbling block to any settlement. The builder's insurance company blamed the architect for 90% of the problems and the latter, having no coverage, could not possibly agree to pay for all the repairs. If both men had been insured it seems more likely our house would have been fixed and a trial avoided.

If our developer had been insured it is even less likely there would have been a trial. Lacking any insurance, the developer perversely denied all responsibility. It seems unlikely that an insurance company would have exposed itself to the risk of recision when our only contract was with the developer.

You need to get in writing that the builder, developer (large or small), or architect is insured and that the insurance will stay in force through the completion of your project. This may be impossible to enforce, but it is nonetheless a good idea.

The other major issue regarding insurance is collectability. You cannot collect from someone who is bankrupt. If the responsible people don't have proper insurance, and you cannot unequivocally cover the project with some other type of structural insurance policy (see No. 6), in my opinion you should avoid the deal. It's not worth the risk. Go elsewhere with your business, even if elsewhere is more expensive.

4. **HIRE A GOOD REAL ESTATE LAWYER.** There are many aspects of any real estate transaction that might require the services of an attorney. Mortgage departments of banks usually handle much of this work, such as arranging for title search and title insurance, and I have not found an attorney absolutely necessary when buying a used house. Remember this, however: the real estate agent represents the seller, not the buyer. When you buy a used house through a real estate agent you have no one representing your interests.

In some states (including Ohio) real estate agents are required by law to have the buyer sign a statement that he/she understands the agent *represents the seller.* If you have any questions of a legal nature, or any doubts about the transaction, you should consult a lawyer.

In any case, I emphatically recommend that you not buy a new house without first consulting a lawyer. Whereas with a used house the seller is moving for some personal reason (new job, bigger house, retirement), the only reason for selling a new house is to generate a profit. It is you against a seasoned businessman. If a real estate agent is involved it is you against *two* seasoned business people. Without a good lawyer you don't have much chance of redress if any conflict arises (with a bad lawyer you have no chance at all).

Here is a worst-case scenario of what can happen when buyer-without-lawyer meets builder-without-scruples. From an article in the Spartanburg Herald, April 24, 1992:

> One of Spartanburg's largest builders...has been indicted by the Spartanburg County grand jury for failing to pay the loan on a house he sold to a retired Michigan couple.
>
> Despite the criminal charge leveled against [the builder], the [homebuyers] may lose the house for which they paid the cash. That's because [the builder] never turned the money over to First Piedmont Federal Savings and Loan of Gaffney, which made him a $79,000 loan.

The article points out how the couple paid the builder $103,000 for the house in four installments, and how the builder turned over only a small part of these funds to the bank. At the time of the article the bank was trying to decide if the couple would be evicted from their home because the builder had not paid the loan. The article also notes:

> ...when the house purchase settled, no attorney was present, but [the builder's associate] gave the [home buyers] the impression she was there on behalf of a law firm.

Having your own attorney will at least reduce the risk of outright fraud, but you need to be protected from far more than that. If you don't already have an attorney expert in real estate transactions, lean toward a member of a sizable law firm, where backup legal help will be available if needed. Do not hire a novice attorney when building a new home. We paid almost $1000 to our contract attorney, yet our contract left us no recourse except protracted and enormously expensive litigation.

Don't use a friend or relative, or any lawyer who ever represented the people you're doing business with. Ditto for the law firm. Do everything possible to make sure your attorney and law firm have *no conflicts of interest.* You should also not use any attorney recommended by your real estate agent or builder. The attorney may do business with the real estate company, or be a friend of the agent or builder. If events turn nasty your lawyer may end up with a conflict. Assume there will be problems, and that you will need your lawyer 100% on your side.

Tell the lawyer you want to be fully protected from the worst: a builder who skips town without finishing your house and leaves you with unpaid subcontractor's bills; or a structurally-defective house that the builder refuses to fix; or a legal judgment against a bankrupt builder. He will say that guaranteed protection from all the worst case scenarios is impossible, which is probably true. Tell him to do his best. As a test, give him a copy of *Crumbling Dreams* and ask him to review this section. I can't tell you what a 'correct response' should be, but if you believe the advice in this chapter is worthwhile, you should be able to tell by the lawyer's attitude toward the book if he's the right counsel for you.

As an example of what a good real estate lawyer can do for you, consider the following. In some states it is possible for unpaid subcontractors (plumbers, electricians, etc.) to put a lien on your house *after* you have moved in and fully paid the builder. In this situation the subcontractors are unpaid by the builder, not by you, but the lien is against your house, not the builder's. In theory, your homeowner's insurance policy or title insurance policy should protect against this problem, but they usually do not; in fact, such insurance policies may specifically exclude the payment of so-called mechanics' liens. Quoting a Washington Post article from March 18, 1991 titled, "Bills Unpaid by Builder Burden Va. Homeowners,"

> Real estate attorney Robert J. Beagan said Virginia home buyers should be sure to ask for mechanics lien coverage and if the insurance company refuses, "you should ask why. If the answer is that the company is not sure all the subcontractors have been paid, you might want to reconsider buying the house."

Chances are, you would never think to ask about mechanics' lien coverage. Why should you? If you paid the builder for your house, how can the plumber he hired for the job come after you for an unpaid bill? But, in some states, unpaid subcontractors can put a lien on your house. If that happens, you cannot sell or refinance your home until these mechanics' liens are fully paid.

Let's face it. Nothing is risk free, least of all building or buying a new house. But a good lawyer will know how to help protect you from the worst. If your lawyer is put off by your concerns, or seems inexperienced in the area of local real estate law, you should obviously look for another attorney.

5. **INSIST ON THE TIGHTEST CONTRACT FEASIBLE FOR YOUR CIRCUMSTANCES.** I don't pretend to tell lawyers how to write a legal contract, nor should you. But every contract should be written as if you will end up in court over it. Judges will ignore your pain and suffering, discount all your expenses, and gloss over lies and verbal assaults made by the builder and his attorney, but they will read the contract. The contract, plus what

the experts say, is likely *all* they will care about in your complaint. This doesn't guarantee a fair decision; remember, the laws in every state favor the builder. But if the contract is well done, you will have a better chance in court than otherwise. Better yet, a clear and unequivocal contract might force a reasonable settlement without having to go to court.

Unfortunately, our contract was so full of holes the developer was able to profit by breaching it. There are clearly some things that should appear in the contract of any prospective new-home buyer that were absent in ours. The whole idea is to ensure the solvency and legal responsibility of the builder, developer, and architect, and to foster resolution of disputes without litigation. Even if the house is properly constructed, you should consult a lawyer for all the myriad financial and legal pitfalls that have nothing to do with defective construction. In the area of new house construction, I recommend the following:

a) Never accept any contract offered by the builder. Even if it seems proper, have it totally rewritten by your attorney. Only then will he think about the meaning and implication of every sentence. If he doesn't think it necessary to re-write the contract, ask him if he agrees with every sentence, and if there is anything that could be construed as ambiguous. About real estate contracts in general, one attorney author wrote:

> I cannot implore you strongly enough to read the entire contract, word for word, and to ask your attorney to explain each and every clause in detail. There are no stupid questions. After all, you are buying the home and signing the agreement, not your attorney. Don't let him get away with saying that a clause is "standard." Remember, yours is a custom deal. (Pollan 1988)

b) Have the contract state who is insured, by whom and for what problems. Although it may be unavoidable, you should not take possession of the house unless the insurance is in force.

c) Include a statement regarding financial solvency of the signers. You want to know that the people building your house are not close to bankruptcy. Some attorneys demand a performance bond from the builder. Others stipulate that a fixed portion of the sale proceeds will be kept in escrow for six months after you move in, returnable with interest to the builder if there are no major defects or disputes. A financially shaky builder will never agree to an escrow arrangement. If you and your attorney cannot ensure that the builder is financially sound, go elsewhere. You don't want to deal with someone who can't meet a payroll, let alone fix your house after you move in.

d) Make the signers of the contract responsible for everything: all "improvements" to the property, including house design, foundation, structural integrity, plus any problems arising from water leakage, improper landfill, etc. Those who sign should be unambiguously responsible for anyone you do not personally contract and pay for. (Remember that our builder's insurance company blamed almost everything on the architect, even though the architect was not hired or paid by us. One sentence in our contract stipulating that the developer and builder were fully responsible for *anyone* they hired might have greatly shortened the litigation process; such a stipulation would have made the architect another subcontractor, instead of an independent — and uninsured — professional.)

e) For a house you are building, or one that is not yet completed, insert a penalty clause to take effect if the house is not completed on schedule. This will require the builder to pay you a certain amount each day beyond the stipulated date of completion. This clause serves two purposes. First, it gives the builder incentive to finish on time. Second, should you be out of your old house before the new one is finished, it provides funds to pay for rent or for a hotel until you can move in.

f) Make title transfer contingent on satisfactory and *independent* review by an architect and/or structural engineer that you hire and pay for. If you are also concerned about environmental problems (e.g., radon gas), add an environmental survey as well.

It is mandatory that you and your expert be allowed to visit the building site at any time during construction. Even though you are buying the house, the builder can legally keep you off the premises until close to the date of completion, unless your contract states otherwise.

With the right inspection clauses in your contract, if you discover the house is not built right before you take title the builder should be legally obligated to fix the problem or refund any down payment. Even if your moving plans are disrupted, it is far better to find out about major problems before title transfers than after *you* own the house.

g) Do not allow the builder to use an occupancy permit as proof that his work is completed. More specifically, your contract should *never* require you to take possession simply because an occupancy permit has been granted. An occupancy permit guarantees nothing about the structural integrity of your home. And remember, inspectors for a municipality are immune from lawsuits (see Section 2).

At the same time, make sure an occupancy permit is granted before you take possession of the house. Except for rural areas, an occupancy permit is required before you move in, yet some builders sell a house without one. Don't get caught buying a house without a valid occupancy permit.

h) Stipulate binding arbitration for any disputes. Binding arbitration is where the disputing parties agree to abide by the decision of an expert panel. Both sides get a chance to present their evidence in an informal setting. If there is something truly wrong with your house the arbitrators will determine what has to be done. If the builder is told to fix something, and does not, a legal judgment will be rendered against him. (Binding arbitration is the one clause most lawyers are surprised we didn't have in our contract).

Ideally, the arbitration panel should include three experts, one chosen by you, one by the builder, and the third mutually agreed upon by all parties. Whether the panel includes one, two or three people, *none* of the arbitrators should be a local contractor or builder, or know your builder socially or professionally. A qualified real estate attorney will be familiar with the proper arbitration process.

The American Arbitration Association provides lists of arbitrators for every aspect of real estate transactions, including home construction. AAA has offices in many cities (check the Yellow Pages in your area). The address and phone number of AAA's national office are listed in the Appendix.

Of all the recommendations I offer in this chapter, mandatory arbitration may be the most controversial. The reason is that many homeowners have been burned by the arbitration process, and wish they had gone to trial instead. Take the case of a Virginia doctor, whose story appeared in Medical Economics, March 6, 1989.

> "My wife and I thought building a new house would make us happy. Instead, it has given us nearly five years of misery. Two mistakes led to our unhappy results. First, we chose the wrong builder, who left our $180,000 home badly flawed. Second, we went to arbitration for a settlement."

The physician then details how he ended up with an unfair arbitrator — a local builder!

> "The hearing was held in the kitchen of our house...The arbitrator's decision came a month later. It was a shock. He ruled against us on all but one of the five major flaws, and his award was inadequate.
> "We've paid $8,000 for repairs, and we'll probably have to spend another $4,000. We won't fix the kitchen or put in new flooring. That would cost $24,000, more than we care to spend.
> "[My wife] says she's lived in the house for nearly five years without being able to enjoy it because an army of engineers, architects, builders, and other people keeps marching through to inspect it and tell us what's wrong with it. Maybe when we finish the repairs, we'll finally be happy in our new home."

Because of horror stories like this one, many lawyers (as well as others) recommend against mandatory arbitration. However, with a proper arbitration process — i.e., a panel of experts who are *not* local builders or connected with the people in your case in any way — the process is bound to be fairer than what this doctor experienced.

The main reason I recommend an arbitration clause is that litigation is extraordinarily expensive and the laws do not allow for reimbursement of legal or experts fees, or for the time you will spend fighting the case. And, winning a legal judgment is no guarantee that you will be paid (see Recommendation No. 10). Yes, a trial and judgment that fully compensate you for repairs, aggravation and expenses would be better than what you are likely to achieve in arbitration. But the former is fantasy, the latter a realistic path to getting your house fixed and minimizing your losses.

The only acceptable substitute for binding arbitration is a contract clause stipulating that the losing side pays legal fees, a stipulation of value *only* if the signer is insured. If you cannot recover legal costs then go with binding arbitration, as long as the process is fair and impartial. If legal fees are not potentially recoverable, and your lawyer won't include an arbitration clause (or the builder won't sign it), show your lawyer Recommendation No. 10. If your lawyer still disagrees, I recommend against buying the house unless, for some reason, you can be certain it will be (or has been) well-constructed. Otherwise, you are leaving yourself highly vulnerable if things go wrong.

6. TRY TO OBTAIN YOUR OWN INSURANCE POLICY FOR DESIGN AND CONSTRUCTION MISTAKES. As discussed in Section 2, builder-offered policies supposedly insure against structural defects for 10 years, but in fact the policies often do not pay for major structural mistakes. I recommend instead that you search for an alternative warranty, which will no doubt be more expensive than a builder-sponsored policy.

Look for a special one-of-a-kind policy that some insurance companies (not builders) may offer. Traditional homeowners' policies cover fire, theft, etc., and specifically exclude defects of design and workmanship. However, a few large companies (Lloyds of London; Chubb Insurance Companies) will write a new-construction policy in some areas. We did not appreciate the need in 1985 for specific structural insurance. Such insurance might have saved us a fortune and years of heartache.

If you are building or buying a new house, call an insurance broker of any large company and tell him you want a policy so that no matter what is wrong with the house, they will pay to both investigate the problem and to fix it according to local building codes. If such a policy exists, consider buying it, even if there is a large deductible of a few thousand dollars. Make sure the policy will pay to fix defects without you having to prove them in court.

The insurance company might offer such a structural-insurance policy as umbrella coverage on top of the builder's own warranty or the builder-sponsored homeowner's warranty (e.g., the HOW). You will have a much better chance of buying such a unique policy before the house is built or before you take title, because then the insurer can inspect the house while it is being built, or at least before you own it. After you move in, such a policy may be much more difficult to buy. In any case, before you buy any structural insurance policy, including the HOW or similar builder-sponsored insurance, have it reviewed by your attorney.

7. MAKE SURE YOUR NEW HOUSE IS NOT BUILT OVER A TOXIC WASTE DUMP. Love Canal. The name brings to mind homes built over a toxic dump, on land too polluted for human habitation. Of course Love Canal refers to a specific place, a neighborhood of Niagara Falls, NY, where homes were built on land previously used for toxic waste disposal. In the 1970s and 1980s Love Canal homeowners became ill from fumes and toxins invading their homes. After much bitter wrangling and mountains of bad publicity, most of the homes were bought back by the federal or state government.

Toxic homes are more common than most people realize; like bad construction, the problem exists all over the country. The entire town of Times Beach, MO was abandoned in 1983 because tests indicated that highway spraying had left high levels of the poison dioxin in the soil. Buy a home built over a toxic dump and you not only have to worry about loss of equity, but also about your and your family's health.

A couple profiled in Money Magazine ("Home Sweet Toxic Home," June 1992, pages 124-139) bought a $91,000 home in a

Savannah, GA subdivision. Defects in the subdivision's 44 houses, such as warped door frames and crooked windows, were ultimately traced by county inspectors to emission of *methane gas*.

Where did the methane come from? Decaying tree stumps, scrap lumber and other debris, dumped in the site a decade earlier, were emitting the gas. Because of the risk of explosion, the entire subdivision was evacuated and the streets sealed off. After investigation 35 of the homes were declared uninhabitable, and the county bought them from the homeowners at fair market value. Nine of the houses — including the one owned by the couple profiled in Money — were deemed safe to live in.

The 'lucky' few homeowners with safe houses were told they could move back. Into what? A ghost subdivision. And houses that had lost half their market value. No way, said these homeowners. Instead, they filed lawsuits against the county and the subdivision's developer.

How common is the toxic waste problem for homebuyers? According to the Money article:

> [The couple] join the growing ranks of Americans who have lost some or all of their home equity to environmental contamination. Nobody knows how many people are in this fix, but the number is almost certainly rising as toxic dumps proliferate. Some 40 million Americans live within four miles of one of the 1235 sites that have made the U.S. Environmental Protection Agency's Superfund National Priority List — sort of the most wanted list of hazardous waste — and about 50 to 100 new sites turn up each year. EPA officials think the toxic tally will eventually reach 1000 sites, but others expect it to go much higher.

What can you do to protect yourself from this nightmare? A lot, depending on how concerned and compulsive you are. Here are a few steps, taken from the Money article and other sources, to make sure your new house is completely safe from toxic wastes.

    a. Hire an expert. Check the yellow pages for "Engineers, Environmental," or call the Phoenix-based Environmental

Assessment Association (602-483-8100) for the name of an expert in your area. This group includes many different types of professionals who know how to survey a house for environmental problems.

b. Obtain a 'chain-of-use' report, which something like a title search on the land. The engineer you hire might be able to do this in addition to surveying the site, or you can consult a real estate attorney. Alternatively, you can be your own sleuth; by searching county records, you should be able to find what the land was previously used for.

c. Check out the surrounding area. An organization called Citizen's Clearinghouse for Hazardous Wastes (119 Rowell Court, P.O. Box 6806, Falls Church, Va 22040) will send you a Neighborhood Toxic Report ($15) that identifies hazardous sites in your zip code. The list is compiled from records of the EPA and other government sources.

d. Test the water, particularly if you have well water. Call your local water department for more information, or National Testing Laboratories (1-800-458-3330).

e. Test for radon. Radon is a radioactive gas given off by natural decay in some areas. Excessive amounts of the gas can cause lung cancer. In recent years many homes have been found to be contaminated. There are two ways to test for radon:

- Do-it-yourself kits approved by the environmental protection agency ($25 to $50). Call the EPA's Radon Hot Line (1-800-SOS-RADON) or your state's Radon Office (every state has one) for a copy of "A Citizen's Guide to Radon," a 15-page brochure that tells what you need to know.

- Pay for a radon survey. Check the yellow pages under Radon for the names of surveyors. You shouldn't spend more than $150 to have an expert test the lot (or your new house) for radon.

If radon is found the house can be fixed, through proper venting, for about $500 to $1500. Your states's Radon Office or the local expert you called can provide more information about radon detection and decontamination.

8. **HIRE INDEPENDENT PROFESSIONALS TO REVIEW THE PLANS, THE CONSTRUCTION, AND THE COMPLETED DWELLING.** *If you follow only one of the recommendations in this chapter, make it this one.* If the architect is paid by the builder or developer, by all means obtain independent review of the plans. If the design is being built for the first time, also hire an independent structural engineer to review the plans. Such a move on our part might have uncovered the inadequate steel beams long before they were installed.

One structural engineer, not involved in our case, told us, "architects are trained to draw pretty houses, not build sound ones." This engineer had testified in cases where the architect's design had been defective. He was dismayed at architects' lack of know-how in building a structurally sound house.

Some may differ with this engineer's assessment but in our case, at least, the architect was demonstrably incompetent in the most important area — design of the supporting steel beams for the house. In this crucial area he did not consult with a structural engineer. Had he done so, I believe we'd still be living in the house today. (That he proved to be dishonest about his role only added to our difficulty. The engineer may be right about architects' general ignorance of structural matters, but I have always admired the profession and was stunned when our architect lied about his mistakes.)

In any case, don't worry about the minor stuff; too many home buyers worry about scratched floors and not the steel beams underneath them. Too many people concern themselves with the finish of the cabinets and not the supporting walls behind them. If you must worry, worry about the structural integrity of your home. You cannot properly check it out yourself, so don't even try. Hire a professional.

If you are building the house, the earlier in the construction process you have an independent inspection, the better. If you wait until after the foundation is completed, it may already be too late (see case of Mr. and Mrs. F, page 83). If you are buying a completed house or condo, make sure you have the house inspected by a qualified engineer before you make any financial commitment. In all cases insist on a written report.

Where do you find the right experts? First, of course, ask your attorney for a recommendation. If he can't recommend the right expert, let your fingers do the walking. Every sizable city has engineers who know how to inspect houses for structural defects. Check the following listings in the Yellow Pages:

"Engineers, Professional"
"Engineers, Consulting"
"Engineers, Structural"

Make several phone calls. Tell the person you speak with exactly what you want and ask how they can help. Ask what the charges are and what you can expect for this money. Eventually you will find someone who seems to have the experience you need and is willing and able to inspect your new house or condominium. Make sure they are not friends or relatives of the builder or anyone connected with constructing your house.

Expect to spend 1/4 to 1% of the cost of the dwelling (not counting land) for an independent structural investigation. If done properly, it will be worth every penny. This extra expense will help ensure the proper construction of your home. If you buy the house during construction, try to visit the site a few times with your independent expert. Ask questions. And make sure you obtain written reports from your expert. No matter how you manage supervision of construction, don't depend solely on your own surveillance. I was at the building site almost daily, for all the good it did. However, if you do see something wrong, speak up. The builder will be most receptive before the house is finished. If the builder is unresponsive to your calls or complaints, consider walking away from the deal. This may not be easy, but consider it anyway. Otherwise you may be in store for future headaches.

Just prior to move-in on any new house, have the structure inspected by a seasoned professional who had nothing to do with its construction or design. It's critical that you hire and pay him. *NEVER* rely on bank or municipal inspectors. Their inspections are a rubber stamp only, a fact that is no secret to anyone who has bought a defective house.

Building codes vary widely across the country, but an occupancy permit from any town or city inspector means the same thing everywhere: the plumbing works and you can move in. Our house was neither designed nor built in accordance with local building codes, but we (and countless other victims of faulty-construction-not-built-to-code) still received an occupancy permit. The title "inspector" for any agent of the bank or municipality is really a misnomer. These people make no attempt, nor do they claim, to inspect for construction, structural, or design defects. And don't forget: the doctrine of sovereign immunity means that neither the municipality nor the inspector can be sued.

9. KEEP DETAILED RECORDS. DOCUMENT EVERY-THING. When it became evident that our builder did not understand the problems with our new house, I began keeping a log of all conversations and interactions with him and his workmen. From the beginning of construction we had saved all the written correspondence about the house (mainly letters and bills), but never dreamed we would end up documenting who said what and when.

If you end up in a dispute, you should expect distortions and alterations of events by the other side. Long before we filed our lawsuit, we realized the builder was distorting the truth about our complaints. At that point (about eight months after we moved in) meticulous documentation became imperative. Subsequently, over a three month period, we wrote four detailed letters to the builder and developer, laying out exactly what the problems were, and how they had not been corrected. These letters served notice that no one could claim ignorance of the problems, or that there was a misunderstanding of our complaints. Along the way we also took numerous pictures of the specific defects.

I can't say all this documentation improved our legal outcome, but it did prevent the defendants from blatantly lying after the lawsuit was filed. It is hard for a builder or developer to say he never heard from you when there is proof he received your certified letters!

Keeping the defendants from lying is only one reason to document everything. Another reason is to keep facts and events straight in your own mind. A year or two later, you are not going to remember who came to fix what, or what the builder said when, and that information may one day be valuable. Detailed records will also make it much easier for your lawyer, should you need one, to understand the history of any dispute you have with the builder.

I recommend you keep a dairy about the house from the moment you start to build or decide to buy. The diary need not be extensive, and may consist of only a sentence or two whenever you have a conversation with the builder or his workmen, or when you visit the construction site. "Spoke with Builder X today. He said the foundation's eight footers will be finished next week."

I also recommend you keep every letter and memo received in chronologic order, either in a three-ring binder or scrap book. Finally, I recommend you (or your independent expert) photograph the construction at every opportunity. Date and label each picture.

All of this documentation can be done unobtrusively. You don't have to be obnoxious or sound threatening. Your aim should simply be to document everything about the house so that, if there is ever a dispute, you have the information you need at your fingertips.

10. **IF AT ALL POSSIBLE, AVOID GOING TO TRIAL.** Avoid going to trial? It must seem strange that you want to build or buy a new house and I'm advising you to keep out of court. That's a little like reading a book on how to play soccer that advises, "avoid going to the hospital."

If you end up with house problems that make you want to haul the builder into court you are, as they say, in deep trouble. That is why I strongly recommend prevention as the first line of defense. The second line is a contract that stipulates binding arbitration against an insured builder. The third line is to do your best to avoid going to court. If you can effect any kind of reasonable settlement, give up the court date. What is a "reasonable settlement" is for you and your attorney to decide, but in the context of civil litigation it will almost always be one where you lose some money.

So why should you avoid trial? Check out anyone victimized by defective construction and you'll find the same aggravations, only different players. Every victim has tales of dishonesty, greed, incompetence, lying, and an appalling lack of integrity. And stories of an indifferent or unfair legal system.

Can you win legally against an irresponsible builder or developer? Can you win financially? What are your chances of coming out ahead, or even whole, by pursuing a lawsuit over defective construction all the way to trial? Unfortunately, your chances are not very good.

In a civil lawsuit your goal is basically monetary: money to get your house fixed, or a fair price from the builder to buy it back, or reimbursement for the cost of repairs. You would also like damages for all the aggravation you've encountered but, realistically, you would be satisfied just to recoup your expenses and enough money to get the house properly fixed. Legally, your case seems straightforward. Builder X constructed your house, it is defective in some major and provable way, and you want it repaired or the house bought back at a fair price. Above all, you certainly don't want to lose money on the house. So you plan to hire a lawyer and sue for redress. Sounds simple enough, right?

Wrong. Very, very wrong. It's not for nothing that Builder X has refused to fix your house or has ignored your complaints. He *knows* you have an uphill legal battle, that the odds are heavily in his favor in any litigation. By refusing to make proper repairs he has said, in effect, "Sue me. See if I care." He probably doesn't. If he is that type of person, he has good reason not to be concerned. Let's look at the steps you must accomplish to achieve proper financial redress in a civil lawsuit against an irresponsible builder or developer. These steps are the same if the builder is or is not insured.

a) Hire a good lawyer. This is not the same type of lawyer in Recommendation No. 4, an expert in real estate contracts. Now you need a litigator, someone who goes to trial. We hired supposedly one of the best litigators in Cleveland. He worked hard on our case, but was frequently befuddled by the tactics of the defendants and their lawyers. During two years of litigation he made several mistakes, including not being fully prepared for the first trial date. All would have been forgiven with a decent outcome, of course, but when the dust settled we found ourselves forced out of our home at a loss of over $160,000. He felt bad about the result, but not as bad as we did.

Every plaintiff who loses money in a civil case wishes he had a better lawyer. So we paid for what we thought was the best and ended up disappointed. What are *your* chances of hiring a good lawyer, an attorney who will consistently do the right thing and not make major mistakes? There are many worse lawyers than the one we had, and no doubt many better ones.

Surprisingly, very few attorneys are knowledgeable in this area. Although the total number of defective houses nationwide is large, the range of possible defects is practically infinite, running the gamut from inadequate design to faulty materials to shoddy workmanship. In the aggregate, thousands of individual companies are responsible. As a result of such diversity, no single attorney or law firm gains expertise in defective construction. You will be lucky to find an attorney with experience in residential real estate litigation.

This situation is in contrast to other major consumer problems, such as defective cars, asbestos-related lung disease and silicone breast implants. In these areas, where only a few companies may be culpable, a handful of law firms gain real expertise in the product and its defects.

If every defective house or condo was built by only a few large companies, the prevalence of defective construction would be a consumer scandal of national proportion. Congress would no doubt become involved. Legislation would be passed. To stay in business, the companies would have to provide 10-year guarantees for each new house. Even then, there would be situations where the few giant companies would dispute claims, or the homeowner would feel cheated by a proposed settlement. (This is close to the situation with new-home warranties, which are dominated by a few large companies; see Section 2.)

Since in every metropolitan area there are dozens to hundreds of defective new homes built yearly, a few law firms in each city would gain experience litigating against Monolithic Builders Corp. or Gigantic Contractors Inc. Buyers of defective construction would have no trouble finding an attorney experienced for their situation.

But such is not the case with home construction. There are thousands of construction companies in the U.S., some big but most small. The small ones are very small, literally one guy who hires a bunch of subcontractors. And the rules by which every house is built vary so much — the contracts, the financing, and the local building codes all have their peculiar twists and turns — that every case of litigation is a new and untrodden path for the lawyer. The result, especially when the lawyer has no experience in this area, is bound to be disappointing to the plaintiff.

I am not anti-lawyer. Indeed, a good attorney can be worth his or her weight in gold when you are up against a dishonest or irresponsible builder. But finding the right attorney for a defective house case is not easy. And *no attorney is better than the wrong attorney.* The wrong attorney can take your money and get you nowhere, as has happened too many times. After falling victim to an incompetent builder you can also fall victim to an incompetent attorney. You have to be very careful.

If you have the money to pursue a legal battle against your builder (a big if), you can increase your chances of success by searching hard for Mr. or Ms. Right Attorney. Try to find other home buyer victims and see if they were satisfied with their litigator. Interview at least two attorneys before making a decision. Ask tough questions. Your choice is a crucial one.

b) File a lawsuit. This is the easy part of litigation. Anyone can file a lawsuit. Builders get sued all the time. For them, it's a ho-hum affair, merely a nuisance action from another unhappy home buyer. For the home buyer, on the other hand, the lawsuit is likely to be a major and traumatizing life event. People certainly never expect to file a lawsuit over their dream home! As you will see, a builder willing to be sued rather than fix your house has very little to lose. You, on the other hand, stand to lose a lot, starting, of course, with money.

First, as plaintiff you have to prove your case. That takes much money and time. You will have legal and experts' fees, plus depositions to pay for, which are horrendously expensive (minimum $2.00 per page, and the pages are typed double spaced with amazingly wide margins). The builder doesn't have to prove anything, but only has to pay his lawyer to delay and deny your claims, actions which don't cost much money. Plaintiffs always spend more than defendants in a civil case. (If the builder is insured the defense's legal well is bottomless.

Perversely, insurance companies seem to prefer paying lawyers money to deny the obvious rather than investigate and properly fix a defective house.)

Second, chances are you have a regular job and any time taken in meetings, depositions, and the trial is time away from work. The builder, however, is a free lance operator; he can take time off whenever he wishes, and likely does not lose money showing up for meetings and depositions.

Third, anything the builder (or insurance company) pays to defend the claim is tax deductible. Your costs are not. To the builder, your house is a business. To you, the house is your home and a personal item; expenses to protect its value are not tax deductible. That's why even uninsured builders would rather go to court than fix a major defect in a single family home. Let's say your house has $30,000 worth of defects, which the builder refuses to fix. You file suit. If your total expenses for attorneys and trial experts come to $25,000, the builder might spend 1/5 of that, or $5,000, *all of which is tax deductible*; his out of pocket expenses (after tax deductions) will be around $3000. So for $3000 he avoids spending $30000. But what about a judgement against him for $30,000? If he is willing to go to court over the money, he is not worried about a judgment (see item g). If he's worried, he'll settle without going to court.

c) <u>Hire competent experts who can give effective testimony in court</u>. Not so easy. In our case, the first builder we hired as an expert witness became confused about his testimony on the eve of deposition, and had to be dropped from the case. (This was our litigator's mistake, since the builder had not been properly prepared for the deposition. This blunder cost us a delay of several months in getting to trial). Also, our first expert engineer was deemed too weak for courtroom testimony, so we had to hire another engineer, which increased out expenses. You will need to find people who are not only expert in your problem area, but also able to give effective testimony in court. Such high quality people will not come cheap. In preparing a solid case for trial expect to spend thousands of dollars for experts.

d) <u>Get to court</u>. In Cleveland it takes 1-2 years to reach court on a civil suit, in other cities a lot longer. Generally, the bigger the city the greater the delay in getting to trial. For one thing, you are competing with hundreds of other cases on any one docket. But even without the backlog in our civil courts, there are so many ways to delay a trial that it's laughable. The defendants can easily delay a year or more by claiming illness, by making phony offers to settle, by requesting records that don't exist, and so forth. In the meantime, while waiting for your day in court, you continue to pay money to your lawyer, and lose both appreciation on your new house and any enjoyment you expected from living in it. The builder, of course, goes right on building.

e) <u>Win a fair decision</u>. You can have a good lawyer, top flight experts, a solid case and still receive an unfair decision. Even when a plaintiff's case is air tight, decisions in civil litigation usually do not work to the advantage of the victim. The reason is simple: In the eyes of the law your complaint is only about a business transaction. Plaintiffs *almost never come out even* litigating a business deal.

The law is the same whether you buy a defective toaster, tractor or new house. What is supposed to be a dream home for you and your family is just a bunch of bricks and wood and mortar in the eyes of the law. You might as well be complaining about a warehouse or barn. You can't recoup legal fees or other money you spend to try the case. Quite often, people win some money to fix their house, but end up spending *as much or more* on legal and experts' fees.

Many victimized homeowners are convinced they can prove fraud in their case: the builder *knew* he was putting in a substandard foundation, the inspector *knew* the house was defective, etc. With a case of fraud, they reason, they will win far more than just the cost of repairs. This, too, is a fantasy. Fraud is extraordinarily difficult to prove in a civil case. Incompetence, stupidity, bad faith, yes. Fraud, no. Check with your lawyer, but in my lay opinion it is not worth going to trial (at your expense) to try to prove fraud. The following is from a news article that appeared in the Los Angeles Times April 5, 1990.

> An unusually bitter lawsuit by nearly three dozen homeowners in Riverside County against [------------] Home Corp. has been settled for about $5.5 million...
>
> The suit by 34 homeowners in Riverside and Corona charged the giant development company with covering up faulty construction methods that caused second-story floors to sag and with paying off a building inspector with gifts. [The company] denied the allegations.
>
> Christopher P. Ruiz, an attorney for the home-owners, said that most of the 34 families are "glad they are finally able to put this behind them"...[He] said some of his clients wanted to try to prove [their] allegations in court. "For the greater good of the group, they elected to accept the settlement," Ruiz said.
>
> ...the litigants were angry over admissions in sworn statements by [the] inspector for the city of Riverside, that he had approved many of the homes without inspecting them and that he had accepted liquor and building materials as gifts from [the company].
>
> [The inspector] denied that the gifts constituted a bribe.
>
> After an extensive investigation [the] Riverside County District Attorney said that there was not enough evidence to warrant prosecution in the case.

I do not know how much this settlement ended up costing the homeowners out of pocket, but I believe they made the right decision by avoiding a trial. My overall impression — from scattered cases around the country, plus talking with attorneys — is that if the local district attorney doesn't think there is enough evidence to pursue a case of fraud, you have little chance of profiting by pursuing fraud in civil court. Always discuss issues like this with your lawyer, of course, but don't lose sight of what should be your main goals: to get your house fixed, recoup as much of your losses as feasible, and end the nightmare.

f) <u>Win on appeal</u>. Let's say you do go to trial and receive a fair decision, i.e., one that fairly compensates you for the house repairs and your expenses. If the builder is insured, expect an appeal by the defense. Appeal to a higher court usually means another year or two delay, plus thousands more in legal fees.

g) <u>Collect a judgment</u>. If you made the mistake of litigating against an uninsured builder, your chances of collecting a judgment are close to zero. Uninsured builders allow themselves to be sued because they don't intend to pay any judgment. This is easy to do by declaring bankruptcy. Bankruptcy is incredibly common among self-employed home builders, who frequently construct each house under a new "corporation." When that corporation is sued it ends up bankrupt. Forget any personal assets in the builder's name. A builder who allows himself to be sued all the way to trial will likely have no personal assets. Assets will be in his wife's name, or in some trust, or hidden in the Cayman Islands. You will have to spend thousands more dollars to find the hidden assets. And even then your chances of collecting will be close to zero.

If the builder is insured you will collect a legal judgment from the insurer, unless the case is appealed once again. Sometimes cases are appealed all the way to the state's supreme court. Let's say you do win, finally, after all the appeals are exhausted. The insurance company pays off, but what do you get? By that point, not much. After a trial and one or two appeals, you will be shocked to learn that legal fees and expenses have eaten up at least half or more of the award. Unless you are one of the rare individuals to take a case through appeals and receive damages (money for pain and suffering), you will likely not receive enough to properly fix your house.

Obviously the legal system is not designed to protect the victimized home buyer. Builders thrive in this system because it is usually cheaper to be sued than to admit mistakes and make major repairs (on a single house, anyway). Don't ever rely on the legal system for protection in a civil case. That will likely be your undoing. You have to protect yourself and, if possible, avoid going to trial. How? Deal only with topflight, reputable people. Work hard to have a good contract that assigns specific responsibility. Pay for professional and independent inspection all the way through construction. Arbitrate disputes.

Prepare for disaster and you will likely move into a well-built, worry-free house.

*   *   *

The recommendations made in this chapter are listed on the next page in tabular form, according to whether you are building a new home or buying one already built. I realize they may seem a lot of bother, perhaps more than any hard-working, non-litigious person cares to consider. They won't be easy to implement and, in the aggregate, could add several thousand dollars to the cost of your new home. However, depending on your own circumstances, all of them may not be necessary.

The goal in all cases is simply to protect yourself and ensure a well-built home, not to scare away competent, honest, responsible home builders. Unfortunately you won't know who is competent, honest and responsible ahead of time. Considering the potential added cost and aggravation if your house is built defectively, anything you spend to prevent problems is worthwhile.

There is one sane alternative, of course. Don't mess with a brand new house. Unless you have deep, deep pockets, or special knowledge about house construction, you just might be better off buying a used home. It's already been lived in and there is no developer, builder, or architect to deal with. That doesn't mean there won't be problems, of course, but at least you can't be disappointed by a builder's empty promises and guarantees.

With the purchase of any used home I also recommend you obtain *three* independent inspections before title transfer: one from a general house inspector, one from a structural engineer, and one from a termite inspector. If the subdivision is new, or the surrounding homes are just a year or two old, you might also want to investigate the land to make sure you're not buying on top of a toxic dump. In any case, you certainly want to avoid the kinds of problems often found with new construction.

It is conceivable that someone who bought a new house, and found it to be defective, is now trying to sell the house after a year or so without proper disclosure (having decided, for obvious reasons, not to fight a legal battle with the builder). Many states

Steps to take when building a new house or buying a new house or condo already built

STEPS	BUILDING A NEW HOUSE	BUYING A NEW HOUSE OR CONDO ALREADY CONSTRUCTED
1 & 2. Check out everyone	Yes; be your own investigator	Yes, but mainly the builder and guarantor of the house
3. Make sure "they" are insured	Yes	Yes; or, alternatively obtain a truly protective structural insurance policy
4. Hire a good real estate lawyer	Definitely	Definitely
5. Insist on the tightest contract feasible	Yes	Yes
6. Obtain your own structural insurance	Yes	Be wary of builder-sponsored structural insurance
7. Investigate the land for toxic wastes	Yes	Yes, although home may only require a visual survey by trained engineer
8. Hire independent experts to review construction, and thoroughly inspect completed house	YES; especially at the start of construction, with emphasis on the foundation and framing 'rough-in'	YES; never buy a new house without a detailed, independent structural inspection that you pay for
9. Document everything	Yes	Yes
10. Avoid going to trial if possible	Yes	Yes

are contemplaing mandatory disclosure laws, but at this writing only Maine and California have them. Whatever your state or community's policy is on disclosure of defects, you can never be too careful.

If you find a used house you like, the price is right, and all inspections are satisfactory, buy it!

Section 5. Some advice for people who design, build and sell new houses, and for other involved parties

> "It is because of the glaring indifference shown by many law enforcement people that some builders have continued to build inferior houses. If officials would get tough, there would be far fewer abuses in home construction."
>
> — A. M. Watkins. *How To Avoid The 10 Biggest Home-Buying Traps*, The Building Institute, 1984

On the chance that this book will find its way to builders, developers, real estate agents, lawyers, politicians, and other people involved in designing, developing, building, selling, insuring, arbitrating and litigating residential real estate, I have some advice.

To builders and developers. The next to last thing homebuyers want is aggravation with their new home. Calling you, bugging you about construction problems, is aggravation. The *last* thing any homebuyer wants is to file a lawsuit, to end up in court over his defective house. My advice is, work hard not to let this happen.

The all important first step, of course, is to build the house right. There is no way I can tell you what to do. You know what to do. Basically, don't cut corners. Make sure the foundation and 'rough-in' are done properly. Most importantly, *care* about your work. A well-built house is a beautiful thing. Care about what you are doing and chances are the house will be well-built. It's when you really don't care that mistakes are apt to occur.

What if there are complaints? Investigate the complaints and try to help the homeowners, not fight them. Call in other experts and be honest about what they find. If there is a problem, fix it right the first time and don't let it languish.

Please don't blame the homeowner when mistakes arise. Blaming others is "externalization". By externalizing the problem to someone else, it becomes easier for you to handle, at least for the moment. But be realistic. Is the homebuyer really responsible for construction mistakes? Doesn't it make more sense to investigate the problem and try to fix it, than to blame the homeowners or some other party?

Don't let your ego get in the way of finding a solution. Everyone makes mistakes: doctors, lawyers, builders. If the house didn't turn out right, the problem should at least be fixable with money and time. It's not as if someone was physically hurt; emotionally, yes, but not physically, so all you have to do is fix the problem and the homeowners should be satisfied. But if you send a junior carpenter to repair a structurally defective foundation with a few pieces of particle board, you *know* it's not going to work.

Don't put your head in the sand. And don't create a situation by which the homeowner has no choice except to file a lawsuit. After all, a lawsuit will cost you something as well. Every dollar you spend on legal fees is a dollar that could solve the problem, and help preserve your reputation. I'm not saying the homeowner is always right, but you shouldn't assume the homeowner is always wrong, either.

Finally, don't make up lies about the complaint. When you lie you engender rage and frustration in the homeowners. Lying, or distorting the truth, destroys your credibility. It shows that you are angry with the homeowners for complaining, and that you are incapable of helping them. Lying hardens the resolve of home-owners to fight you, which is not at all what they want. They want your help, not your anger.

The attitude of builders and developers caught in their mistakes too often seems to be: 'The homeowners are bastards. They are crazy people, you can't satisfy them. They are nuts.' But think: after spending hundreds of thousands of dollars on a new home, why would the homeowners wish to incur aggravation and frustration? None of your customers is asking for a fight. They just want what you promised to deliver, no more and certainly no less. They complain only because something is wrong with their house, not because they are bad people. They will pursue the complaint only if you don't act to fix the house you built.

In summary: Assume the homeowner's complaints are legitimate unless you can prove otherwise with independent, objective evaluations. Investigate the complaints honestly. Work with the homeowners. Don't make up lies or twist the truth for self-serving purposes. And above all, don't call your lawyer unless you have no other choice.

To architects. Don't assume you know it all. Your biggest collective sin may be arrogance. Don't make a mistake with the foundation, the footers, the steel beams, or anything else that can affect the house's structural integrity. Consult a structural engineer, especially if the house has never before been built. Please understand that homebuyers want and deserve more than just a pretty design.

To housing inspectors. Some of your peers have been accused of being dishonest, of accepting bribes to pass on defective construction. I believe that situation is rare, and that most mistakes made by housing inspectors are honest ones, not a result of some builder's bribe. So what should the typically honest inspector do? For starters, be thorough and forthright. If you see a problem, speak up. It will only hurt the homeowners in the long run if you remain silent. Don't worry about missing the small stuff. Are there enough footers? Are they placed in the proper positions? Are the steel beams the right strength for the load they carry? Are the horizontal beams level? Was mortar used to cement the foundation blocks together?

In addition to plumbing and electrical systems, look at the walls and floors; are they straight, and if not, why not? Check for the structural integrity of the dwelling. Above all, think of the people who will move into the house you are inspecting; they are probably no different from you and your family. Don't make it possible for the builder to sell them a lemon.

<u>To real estate agents</u>. Apply the golden rule: treat the home-buyers as *you* would wish to be treated. Don't hide anything. Be honest with yourself, and your clients, and over time you will enjoy a very good reputation. Above all, recommend that buyers of new construction have the house or condo inspected by an independent structural engineer before title transfers.   When people ask why, recommend they read *Crumbling Dreams*. They will be impressed by your concern for their welfare.

<u>To home warranty insurers</u>. It is difficult to know what to make of your industry. Your warranties seem to boil down to what's in the fine print, and damn the homeowners. When you state that there is widespread misunderstanding about what your policies cover, whose fault is that?   If your 'structural insurance' warranties don't cover homes with structural defects — construction that doesn't meet local building codes — is that fact made plain to the homebuyers?   I suggest you re-write your policies so that homeowners understand what they are *not* buying. For example, you might state in bold print that the warranty will only pay for defects up to $3,000, $4,000, or whatever your unwritten limit is. The plain fact — as is apparent to anyone who reads the many stories about litigation against home warranty companies — is that too many people buying your product are not getting the protection they think they are.

The way you do business has attracted the attention of Congress. Before Congress tries to regulate the home warranty business, wouldn't it be simpler for you to revamp how your policies are presented to homebuyers?

Here is another suggestion. Offer a "super policy" that *does cover* major structural defects. This super policy should guarantee — without argument or litigation — repair of *any* construction problem that does not meet local building codes. We would have bought such a policy, and I'm sure many other homeowners will.

You could have a Class A and Class B policy. Class B would be very limited, covering minor defects only, up to a few thousand dollars — apparently what your current policies offer in fact, if not in plain language. Class A would be unlimited, covering all defects — what many homebuyers think they are getting with your current policy, but clearly are not. Figure out what you will have to charge to offer a Class A policy, stand behind it without giving homebuyers a run around, and you will have a lot of takers.

<u>To lawyers representing builders and developers</u>. The non-lawyer public is not too happy with the legal profession. If you wonder why, read some of the books in the last category of the Bibliography. At the grass roots level you can work to change that poor image. When a builder calls you in because of an unhappy homebuyer, don't automatically assume the homebuyer is a nut case. Don't write letters criticizing the homebuyer. Those knee-jerk letters are a cheap shot, and totally unnecessary; if anything, they reflect your own feelings of inadequacy.

Before you heap calumny upon the plaintiffs, have their complaints investigated professionally. By investigating the problems, instead of reflexively fighting the plaintiffs, you will actually help your builder client in the long run. You might not make as much money getting a complaint settled early, but in the long run you will gain a better reputation and probably do better financially, as more and more builders hear about how efficient and reasonable you are.

We know of a lawyer who represented a builder in a defective construction lawsuit. He treated the homeowner plaintiffs in an unnecessarily hostile and combative fashion. When the construction case finally settled out of court, this lawyer was stiffed by his builder client for a huge legal fee. Believe it or not, the lawyer then phoned the plaintiffs, asking if they would testify that he, the lawyer, had actually done the work that generated his legal fees! You can imagine how the plaintiffs responded. I am sure the lawyer wishes he hadn't been so nasty to them.

<u>To lawyers representing unhappy homeowners</u>. Don't take the case if you know of any conflicts, even if they are minor. Do you play golf with the builder's brother? That's a conflict. If you don't think you can adequately represent the plaintiffs all the way through the appeals process, don't take the case. If you don't feel some sense of outrage over their plight, don't take the case.

Be honest with yourself and with your clients. Homeowners who call you about a construction problem are experiencing tremendous frustration. Don't add to their problem. Bow out if you are not the right attorney for them.

If you do take the case, tell the homeowners up front what their chances are of winning *and* collecting. Let them decide if the case is worth pursuing. Give them a maximum figure that they can expect to spend, and offer to take anything over that on a contingency basis. A bottomless legal bill is a hard nut to swallow for people who have just bought a new house.

To arbitrators in construction cases. Don't arbitrate the case if you know the defendants professionally or socially, or if you also build houses in the same area. Be fair in your deliberations. Remember that the house has to meet local construction codes to be salable. Your arbitration should lead to repairs that conform to these codes. A patchwork repair is not fair to the homeowners. Ask yourself what *you* would want done if *you* owned the house.

To judges in construction cases. You are charged with treating plaintiffs and defendants equally before the law. The problem is that the law is stacked heavily against victims of defective construction. They lose the moment they are forced to file a lawsuit. By the time they enter your courtroom they have lost even more. You know that plaintiffs' legal costs are not recoverable. You know that plaintiffs' costs to litigate are not part of doing business, and therefore are not tax deductible. You know that damages are almost never awarded, even though the trauma experienced by homeowners may as great, or greater, than in tort cases.

Understand that the plaintiffs have already incurred great expense in just getting to your courtroom. Understand that no homeowners in their right mind want to be in your courtroom fighting their builder, and that the case is a unique and traumatizing experience for them. On the other hand, builders (or their lawyers) appear in your courtroom all the time.

Within the law, try to treat the plaintiffs fairly. At the same time, don't reward defendants who have clearly lied, breached their contract, or given homebuyers an unnecessary run around. There may be no legal penalty for such behavior, but you have a societal obligation not to reward builders, developers and architects who have displayed unethical and dishonest behavior. When you ignore these transgressions you are indirectly rewarding the people who caused the problems.

Is there nothing you can do a about a builder who defaults on a judgment by declaring a phony bankruptcy? Is there nothing you can do about a licensed professional who lies about his mistakes? Is there nothing you can do about a developer who knowingly tries to sell a defective house without proper disclosure?

To local government officials. Revise inspection procedures to make them tougher. Don't wait for another Seville Place to review your home inspection practices. If necessary, hire more inspectors. And give them sufficient training to do the job properly.

Your natural reflex seems to be to side with the builder or developer in any dispute. Perhaps it is because the builder or developer creates jobs and pours money into the local economy. But are you not elected by the public? Who is your real constituency?

If you are asked for help by someone who finds their new house was not built in accordance with local building codes, don't put your head in the sand. Investigate the complaint. You might be helping many more people — and ultimately securing many more votes — by thoroughly and honestly investigating a home-buyer's complaint. And you will win a friend for life.

To state legislators. The laws are unfair in every state. Can't you change the laws in your state, to provide the homebuyer a fair outcome in a construction dispute? The ball's clearly in your court. Here are some suggestions.

- Make reasonable legal and experts' fees recoverable if the homeowner wins a court case over defective construction.

- Establish a builder-sponsored fund to reimburse homeowners who win a court case against a bankrupt builder.

- Require that every new home not be sold unless it is accompanied by a document stating when it was inspected, by whom, and exactly what was found. This document — what the founder of the Ridgemere Institute refers to as a "purple book" detailing every inspection — should be given to the homeowners along with the occupancy permit.

- Eliminate sovereign immunity for local government inspectors. Physicians who work for state and county hospitals can be sued for malpractice. Why shouldn't homeowners be allowed to sue for inspection malpractice?

- Don't allow bankrupt builders who owe money as a result of a legal judgment to hide assets and keep right on building.

Many other people have suggestions for legal reform at the state level. To obtain more ideas, I suggest you consult attorneys who have represented homebuyer plaintiffs in court. You can write me for a list. Also, call the United Homeowners Association, the North Carolina Homeowners Association, or the Ridgemere Institute (see Appendix). The people who run these organizations have many sound ideas.

To members of Congress. You have some input into new houses backed by federally-guaranteed mortgages. For such construction I have three recommendations; two of them would require new federal laws:

- Don't allow title transfer of any house backed by a federally-guaranteed mortgage that hasn't been inspected for structural defects. Every new house sold should be accompanied by the "purple book" listing dates of inspection, who did the inspections, and what was found.

- If a new house with a federally-backed mortgage is proven structurally defective in court, the government should offer to buy the house back at a fair market price, plus pay all legal fees of the homeowners. To recoup its costs, the government should then sue the builder or other culpable party. The U.S. government will have a much better chance of recovering a judgment than any individual homeowner.

● Perhaps the most immediate step Congress can take is to investigate the extent of the problem. Input from people all over the country might help you pass laws to give the homebuyer some meaningful protection. Don't worry about scaring people away from buying new houses, or hurting the economy. Everyone wants a house of their own. If you figure out a way to financially protect innocent homebuyers against bad builders, more people will buy houses, not less.

<u>To all</u>. Recommend this book to anyone contemplating building or buying a new house or condominium. Better yet, give them a copy. And if you think of anything important I left out, or want to send along information that might be used in a new edition, please write me in care of the publisher.

Section 6. Bibliography: An annotated listing of books to help you build or buy a well-constructed new house (or condo)

My husband and I have examined well over 100 consumer-oriented books about how to buy, build, design, inspect, contract for and otherwise acquire a new house or condominium. Very few of these books discuss the risks and consequences of defective construction. Still, we can recommend many books for the information they provide on practically all other aspects of home building and buying.

Most of the books listed herein, as well as many others like them, can be found in any public library. A new title not in the library can be ordered through any book store, or your library may order it if you ask.

I don't recommend you build any house "by the book." However, the more you know, the more right questions you can ask. All of the listed books have something useful to offer. The best ones for you will depend on your route to a new home — building it yourself, hiring someone to build it, buying it new, or purchasing a used or renovated house.

*   *   *

I have listed the books under two broad categories: 1) Design and construction of a house you plan to build or have built for you, and 2) Inspection and purchase of a new house or condominium that is already built. Books in the second group also discuss the purchase of a used house.

A third category of books, beginning on page 158, has nothing to do with houses per se, but everything to do with business ethics in America. Notice how often words like "greed," "thieves" and "liars" end up in the title of these books.

DESIGN AND CONSTRUCTION OF A HOUSE YOU PLAN TO BUILD OR HAVE BUILT FOR YOU

Burch, Mark. *Complete Guide to Building Log Houses.* Sterling Publishing Co., New York; 1990.
> This large paperback contains many drawings and photographs. See also book by Duncan on this subject.

Daniels, Charles J. *Dream House, Real House. The Adventures of Planning and Building a Custom House.* Macmillan Publishing Co., New York; 1989.
> Daniels is an architect who designed his own home, then hired a builder to construct it. Both this book and the one by Wasfi (below) are for those who plan to design and/or manage construction of their home. You can save a bundle if you know how to do it.

DiDonno, Lupe and Phyllis Sperling. *How to Design and Build Your Own House,* 2nd Ed. Alfred A. Knopf, New York; 1987.
> A large workbook-type manual. Contains many detailed drawings.

Duncan, S. Blackwell. *Build Your Own Log Home From Scratch,* 2nd ed. Tab Books, Blue Ridge Summit, PA; 1988.
> A primer for anyone planing to build his own log home. The author explains both the advantages and disadvantages of log homes. See also book by Burch on this subject.

Ennis, Perry. *Understanding Home Construction. A Complete Layman's Guide to Home Building and Saving Money by Self-Contracting.* Southeastern Publishing Co., 2462 Stantonsburg Rd., Greenville, NC 27858.
> Like many other authors of "how-to-build" books, author Ennis built his own house. His emphasis in this book is on saving money during construction.

Folds, John and Roy Hoopes. *Everything You Need To Know About Building the Custom Home. How To Be Your Own General Contractor.* Taylor Publishing Co., 1550 West Mockingbird Lane,

Dallas, Texas 75235; 1990.
Books of this genre seem to fall into two categories: with and without pictures/diagrams. This one is without, but it offers plenty of useful information. The first author is a real estate attorney, the second an editor who built his own home.

Hamilton, John S.M. *The Working Woman's Dream House. A Design, Building, and Remodeling Guide.* Betterway Publications, Inc. P.O. Box 219, Crozet, VA 22932; 1989.
Covers both building and remodeling, with emphasis on making the home more "beautiful and efficient" for the working woman (including the full time homemaker). The architect author argues for the woman's active involvement in the process, whether it is remodeling or building from scratch. Mentions importance of checking out the architect and builder thoroughly, before even asking for bids.

Hodgins, Eric. *Mr. Blandings Builds His Dream House.* Academy Chicago Publishers, Chicago; 1987.
A work of fiction, *Dream House* was first published in 1946, later made into a popular motion picture starring Cary Grant and Myrna Loy (available on videocassette). Mr. Blandings and his wife build their dream house in the country and run into many complications. The types of characters they meet and their unfortunate experiences seem real enough, but the tone of the book — wry humor — is not true to life.

Kidder, Tracy. *House.* Houghton-Mifflin Co., Boston; 1985.
Pulitzer prize-winner's best seller about construction of a single-family home in Massachusetts. To learn about good builders and quality construction, read this book. Also published in paperback by Avon Books, New York.

Locke, Jim. *The Well-Built House. Everything you need to know before you have a new house built or an old one remodeled.* Houghton-Mifflin Co., Boston; 1988.
By one of the men who built the house in *House*. Useful mainly if you plan to do your own contracting. Concentrates on construction, not financial or legal matters.

Marchiony, William. *The New House Buyer's Guide*. Carefree Living Co., 2509 Thousand Oaks Blvd., #160, Thousand Oaks, CA 91362-3249; 1986.
> This large size paperback is written in workbook style, and offers some very useful advice, plus an extensive glossary of building terms. Alone among all books we reviewed, this guide provides a list of states that require contractors to be licensed (as of the mid 1980s).

McGuerty, David L. and A. Kent Lester. *The Complete Guide to Contracting Your Home*. Betterway Publications, Inc. P.O. Box 219, Crozet, VA 22932; 1986.
> Contains many useful checklists for getting the job done. Also contains a few diagrams and line drawings.

McLaughlin, Jack. *The Housebuilding Experience*. Van Nostrand Reinhold Co., New York; 1981.
> The author built his own house and later published this book, which is about how you can build your own house. "If you are just thinking about building a home, you are part of a growing movement to combat high prices, shoddy workmanship, and the assembly-line sameness of the contractor-built home."

Ortho's Basic Home Building. An Illustrated Guide. Jill Fox, Project Editor; Ron Hildebrand, Writer. Ortho Books, Division of Chevron Chemical Corp., 6001 Bollinger Canyon Rd., San Ramon, CA 94583; 1991.
> A glossy hardcover with full-color illustrations.

Owen, David. *The Walls Around Us*. Villard Books, New York; 1991.
> Tells how a house works in clear, lucid style. Offers many suggestions on what to incorporate if you are building.

Petrocelly, Kenneth L. *Before You Build. 100 Home-Building Pitfalls to Avoid*. Tab Books, Blue Ridge Summit, PA; 1991.
> Discusses many pitfalls. A real estate contract is more complicated than most people assume, and author discusses

it as a potential pitfall. Like almost all books, however, there is no discussion of consequences of defective construction.

Rybczynski, Witold. *The Most Beautiful House in the World*. Penguin Books, New York; 1989.
    The author, a professor of architecture at McGill University, writes of his experiences building a boat house/home. Along the way he discusses architectural history and theory. Not a how-to primer but just a good read. Was a best seller.

Syvanen, Bob. *Tips and Tricks for Evaluating New Construction*. Globe Pequot Press, 138 W. Main St., Chester, CT 06412; 1990.
    An excellent paperback manual by a master carpenter. Includes numerous line drawings on what to look for in new construction, from the foundation up.

Taylor, J. Rodney. *So You Want To Build A House. How To Be Your Own Contractor*. Betterway Publications, Inc. P.O. Box 219, Crozet, VA 22932; 1991.
    Contains lots of how-to information, but no pictures or diagrams.

Vila, Bob, with Jane Davison. *This Old House. Restoring, rehabilitating, renovating an Older House*. Little, Brown, Boston; 1987.
    Restoration has about as many pitfalls as building from scratch, perhaps more. This book is based on the popular, Emmy-award winning PBS television series hosted by Mr. Vila.

Youssef, Wasfi, Ph.D. *Building Your Own Home. A Step-by-Step Guide*. John Wiley & Sons, Inc., New York; 1988.
    An encyclopedic approach to the subject, by a consulting structural engineer. Chapters range from "Buying a Lot" through every aspect of construction to "Certificate of Occupancy and Tax Assessment."

INSPECTION AND PURCHASE OF A NEW HOUSE OR CONDOMINIUM THAT IS ALREADY BUILT

Catalano, Joe. *J.K. Lasser's Guide to Buying Your First Home.* Simon & Schuster, New York; 1991.
   A general guide. Discusses importance of finding the right lawyer in a chapter titled "Choosing a Good Attorney."

Connolly, William G. *The New York Times Guide to Buying or Building a Home.* Times Books, New York; 1984.
   Connolly recommends you get very specific when buying a new house from a developer. "In general, you'll find the developer less flexible than the individual seller of an older home. He's more likely to be willing to see you walk away, less likely to let you have the contract you want. But there's nothing wrong with your accepting the developer's terms, within reason, as long as you know the risk you're taking. Weigh the risk against the benefit — this home rather than some other one — and make your choice. It's your money and your life." Well said.

Dubois, Maurice. *Home Buyer's Confidential. The Insider's Guide to Buying Your Dream House, Condo, or Co-Op.* Liberty Hall Press (McGraw Hill), New York; 1991.
   Dubois is a Dallas-Ft. Worth area real estate expert. The cover advertises what builders (and real estate agents, sellers, and banks) "don't tell you." Inside is a short, no-nonsense chapter, "Buying from Builders," that contains some very useful advice.

Hughes, Alan. *First Time Home Buyers' Guide. Making the Most of the Best Mortgage Rates.* Acropolis Books Ltd., 13950 Dark Center Rd., Reston, VA 22071; 1987.
   This interesting book contains information on log houses, dome houses, factory-built frame houses, mobile & manufactured homes, and rehabilitating a "fixer upper". Emphasis is on the homebuyer's first house.

Irwin, Robert. *Tips and Traps When Buying a Home.* Mc-Graw Hill Publishing Co., New York; 1990.
Covers all the angles and gives some particularly good advice in the chapter "Buying a New Home from a Builder."

Kiplinger's Buying & Selling A Home. By the Staff of Changing Times Magazine. Kiplinger Books, Washington, D.C.; 1990.
A good resource book, covering all the aspects. Briefly discusses limitations of homeowners warranties, which are bought through member builders. Notes that Homeowner Warranty Corporation, one of the nation's largest warranty companies, "has no authority to get tough on delinquent builders except by expelling them from the program. An expelled builder can still go on constructing homes unless stopped by local or state regulatory authorities."

Lank, Edith. *The Homebuyers Kit.* Dearborn Financial Publishing Inc., Chicago; 1991.
Discusses most aspects of home buying, with emphasis on buying a used house.

Madorma, James. *The Home Buyer's Inspection Guide.* Betterway Publications, Inc. P.O. Box 219, Crozet, VA 22932; 1990.
Emphasizes problems that could "arise in the future due to existing conditions...Potential problems are not reasons to forgo a purchase if, and only if, you have been prepared to deal with them." Contains several clear line drawings that show what to look for. Also includes several home inspection checklists.

Makeower, Joel. *How To Buy a House.* The Putnam Publishing Group, New York; 1990.
Paperback book that comes as "2-in-1"; other half of book is *How To Sell a House.* Nothing specific on new houses, but includes some useful inspection and financing information. Useful if you are going to buy and sell at the same time.

Milko, George. *Real Estate. The Legal Side of Buying a House, Condo, or Co-op: A Step-by-Step Guide.* Random House, New

York; 1990.

A paperback that is part of the Random Law Manuals. Milko offers specific advice in many areas, including home owner warranties on new construction.

Minardi, John A. and James A. Minardi. *The Do It Yourself Home Inspection Book. Making Sure Your Investment is Safe and Sound.* Probus Publishing Co., Chicago; 1991.

I am skeptical of using do-it-yourself inspections as the sole check on construction, and would rather trust the job to a professional I can trust. Still, you can't go wrong knowing the information in this and other home inspection books. Books like this should inform you about what questions to ask, and what to look for.

Pollan, Stephen, Mark Levine and Michael Pollan. *The Field Guide to Home Buying in America.* Simon & Schuster, New York; 1988.

Although this book is oriented toward buying used houses, I highly recommend it for the common sense discussion of real estate contracts. The senior author is an experienced real estate lawyer, and the book reflects his expertise. *Field Guide* (and Watkins's *Home-Buying Traps*) should be at the top of any reading list (after my book, of course).

Scutella, Richard M. and Dave Hecherle. *Home Buyers Checklist.* Tab Books, Blue Ridge Summit, PA; 1991.

Contains numerous checklists and line drawings of what to look for, from the ground up.

Sumichrast, Michael. *The New Complete Book of Homebuying.* Bantam Books, New York; 1990.

Discusses arguments for buying a used or new house, plus much financial and tax information.

Thomsett, Michael C. and the Editors of Consumer Reports. *How To Buy a House, Condo, or Co-Op. Basic Strategies and Advice for Evaluating, Financing, and Purchasing a Home.* Consumer Reports Books, Mt. Vernon, NY; 1990.

This Consumer Reports book is aimed predominantly toward buyers of used homes. Recommends hiring both termite and regular home inspectors.

Vila, Bob with Carl Oglesby. *Bob Vila's Guide to Buying Your Dream House*. Little, Brown and Company, Boston; 1990.
Vila is the former host of Public Television's "This Old House," and an acknowledged expert. Emphasis is on purchasing a used home.

Ventolo, William L. *The Complete Home Inspection Kit*. Dearborn Financial Publishing Inc., Chicago; 1990.
Contains specific information on examining homes for both radon and asbestos.

Watkins, A.M. *How to Avoid the 10 Biggest Home-Buying Traps*. Dearborn Financial Publishing Inc., Chicago; 1988.
Contains a chapter creatively titled "The Vanishing Builder" that gives examples (with pictures) of defectively-constructed houses. Watkins is one of the very few authors whose work reflects awareness of the devastation that results when you buy a defectively constructed house. (He once wrote an article on the subject for the Saturday Evening Post that was roundly criticized by the home builders' trade association.) This book (along with Pollan's *Field Guide*) should be at the top of any reading list.

Watkins, A.M. *The Complete Guide to Factory-Made Houses*. Dearborn Financial Publishing Inc., Chicago; 1988.
The author of *10 Biggest Home-Buying Traps* offers a wealth of information on factory-made houses. These structures are built in a factory but assembled on-site.

BUSINESS AND LAW IN AMERICA — A SHORT, HIGHLY SELECTIVE LIST OF BOOKS ABOUT BUSINESSMEN, LAWYERS, AND THEIR CHICANERIES (see pages 95-96)

Adams, James R. and Douglas Frantz. *A Full Service Bank: How BCCI Stole Billions Around the World.* Pocket Books, New York; 1992.
> The story behind the Bank of Credit and Commerce International, the bank that engaged in money laundering, fraud and insider lending for arms merchants, dictators, the CIA, drug traffickers, terrorists and other lawbreakers, and was shut down in July 1991. Before its demise BCCI swallowed the money of depositors in 73 countries. See also the book by Potts in this list.

Auletta, Ken. *Greed and Glory on Wall Street. The Fall of the House of Lehman.* Random House, New York; 1986.
> One of many recent books on Wall Street Greed. Greed is partly what sunk us in our house deal, and what sinks many other home buyer victims.

Bruck, Connie. *The Predators' Ball. The Inside Story of Drexal Burnham and the Rise of the Junk Bond Traders.* Penguin Books, New York; 1988.
> Read this one for the rise. Read Don Stewart's book for the fall.

Burrough, Bryan and John Helyar. *Barbarians at the Gate.* Harper & Row, New York; 1990.
> Another best seller, this one about the leveraged buyout of RJR Nabisco, a billion dollar deal engineered by a group of takeover "artists."

Chase, C. David. *Mugged on Wall Street.* Simon and Schuster, New York; 1987.
> The advertising blurb for this book says it all: "An insider (previously V.P. of EF Hutton Brokerage) shows you how to protect yourself and your money from the financial pros."

Derber, Charles. *Money, Murder, and the American Dream. Wilding form Wall Street to Main Street.* Faber and Faber, New York; 1992.

Wilding is the term for random violence by prowling inner city youth gangs. This book concentrates on selfish economic behavior that harms others. Although the infamous are dealt with here — Milken, Trump, et. al. — Derber also discusses the un-famous, those people who prey on innocents far from Wall Street.

Fay, Stephen. *Beyond Greed.* The Viking Press, New York; 1982.

This book is about how "the two richest families in the world, the Hunts of Texas and the House of Saud, tried to corner the silver market — how they failed, who stopped them, and why it could happen again." As in many other stories, the key word is greed.

Grutman, Roy and Bill Thomas. *Lawyers and Thieves.* Simon and Schuster, New York; 1990.

Grutman, a famous trial lawyer, has come up against some pretty shady lawyers in his day. "Many people today who hire lawyers come away with the experience shaking their heads in disbelief at how they have been bilked, mistreated and ill served. Attorneys are not good samaritans. Some may take pleasure in helping their fellow man, but not many even pretend to do it for free. Enter any courtroom in America and you enter a theater where money talks, where fact and fiction are interchangeable and winning or losing depends on which side hires the best actor."

Kumble, Steve. *Conduct Unbecoming: the Rise and Ruin of Finley, Kumble.* Caroll & Graf, New York; 1990.

An insider's chronicle of the breakup of Finley, Kumble, an aggressive, 700-lawyer firm that, according to Time Magazine, "became synonymous with '80s style greed."

Lewis, Michael. *Liar's Poker.* W.W. Norton Co., New York; 1989.

About the Salomon Brothers brokerage firm and Wall Street

shenanigans. A prescient book, *Liar's Poker* was published before Salomon admitted to violating U.S. Treasury regulations in its handling of bond sales, and before its chairman was forced to resign.

Mayer, Martin. *The Builders. Houses, People, Neighborhoods, Governments, Money.* W.W. Norton & Co., New York; 1978.
An encyclopedic review of everything the title indicates. Although dated, the book provides interesting historical perspectives on many aspects of single- and multi-family construction.

Mayer, Martin. *The Greatest Ever Bank Robbery. The Collapse of the Savings & Loan Industry.* Charles Scribner's Sons, New York; 1990.
Explains the origins and execution of the Savings and Loan thefts of the 1980s. Here we are talking about billions of dollars and the demise of hundreds of S&Ls. Although all the depositors were insured (up to $100,000), the latest estimate is that *every* American (man, woman, child) is in hock about $2000 for this systematic thievery.

Mayer, Martin. *Stealing the Market. How the Giant Brokerage Firms, With Help From the SEC, Stole the Stock Market From Investors.* Basic Books, New York; 1992.
Mayer is a master chronicler of big-theme stories about money, banking and investments. In this book he argues that in recent years stockbrokers have become adversaries of the very customers they purport to serve, mainly by withholding information of the companies whose stocks they sell. This is a complex book whose message boils down to this: in the buying and selling of stocks the playing field is not even; the little guy doesn't have much of a chance.

Pilzer, Paul Zane, with Robert Deitz. *Other People's Money. The Inside Story of the S&L Mess.* Simon & Schuster, New York; 1989.
One of several books on the subject. "How bad luck, worse judgment and flagrant corruption made a shambles of a $900 billion Industry." Also see the S&L book by Martin Mayer.

Potts, Mark, Nicholas Kochan and Robert Whittington. *BCCI —The Inside Story of the World's Sleaziest Bank.* National Press Books, Washington; 1992.

The authors are journalists who cover the same territory as the book by Adams and Frantz: the criminal actions of Bank of Credit and Commerce International or, as Robert Gates, Director of the Central Intelligence Agency, once called it, "the Bank of Crooks and Criminals International."

Rothchild, John. *Going for Broke. How Robert Campeau Bankrupted the Retail Industry, Jolted the Junk Bond Market, and Brought the Booming Eighties to a Crashing Halt.* Simon and Schuster, New York; 1991.

Among the giant retail companies forced into Chapter 11 by this business fiasco were Federated (Bloomingdale's and other stores) and Allied (Brooks Brothers, Jordan Marsh, and other stores).

Spence, Gary. *With Justice for None. Destroying an American Myth.* Times Books, New York; 1989.

Spence, a famous trial lawyer, has a simple message: Unless Americans are wealthy or powerful enough to buy it, they rarely experience true justice. This book hit home with me.

Stein. *A Feast For Lawyers.* M. Evans and Company, New York; 1989.

The author had his own New York publishing company, Stein and Day, which, through no fault of his own, was forced into bankruptcy. His experience in court was, in its own parallel way, as frustrating and demoralizing as was ours. The myth of "bankruptcy protection" reminds us of the myth of "construction guarantees."

Stewart, Don. *Den of Thieves.* Simon and Schuster, New York; 1991.

A best seller about the Levine/Boesky/Milken/Drexal scandal of the late 1980s. The story is exquisitely detailed. If you have not already read this book, you will be shocked to learn what really happened.

Appendix. A few worthwhile organizations

If you have a problem, start locally. To find out if your builder is licensed, or if a license is required, contact your state's licensing board. To find out about your rights under the law, contact the Consumer Protection Division (every state has one) or the state attorney general's office, and make your complaint. Beyond this — and the obvious step of contacting an attorney — are a precious few consumer-oriented organizations that might be able to help in a general way. They can give you some leads on who to call about your particular problem, and perhaps other useful information as well.

United Homeowners Association
805 15th St., N.W., Suite 310
Washington, D.C. 20005
Phone: 1-800-787-HOME or 202-408-8842

A 5000-member trade group that champions the rights of all homeowners. Founder Jordan Clark says he "discovered there are 11,000 organizations in this city and not one was for the homeowner. So I started one." For $12 a year membership you receive a newsletter and access to a wide range of benefits.

North Carolina Homeowners Association
P.O. Box 458, Carrboro, NC 27510-0458
Phone: 919-859-2711 or 919-967-1407.

By far the best state organization of its type. NCHA's officers are willing to give advice and information to callers from other states.

American Homeowners Foundation
1724 S. Quincy St.
Box 4709
Arlington, VA 22204
1-703-979-4663

Provides standard homeowner/remodeler contracts ($5.95 for the first copy, additional copies $1.95 each). Also publishes three inexpensive books, one each on buying, selling and investing in real estate.

Ridgemere Institute
P.O. Box 8247
Historic Hermitage, TN 37076
Phone: 615-885-0101
Fax: 615-889-7066

> The Ridgemere Institute is a non-profit organization co-founded by Mrs. R. Jean Fisher, a Tennessee homeowner who experienced problems collecting on a homeowners warranty policy. The Institute functions as a clearinghouse for information and complaints about home warranty companies. One of the Institute's stated goals is "the regulation by the Federal Trade Commission in the operation of all ten year home protection plans."

The Building Institute
127 S. Broadway
Nyack, N.Y. 10960
Phone: 914-353-4286

> Publishes consumer-oriented books about building and buying houses. Published the 1984 edition of *How to Avoid the 10 Biggest Home-Buying Traps* by A.M. Watkins.

American Arbitration Association
140 West 51st Street
New York, N.Y. 10020-1203
(212)-484-4041

> This organization seeks to provide impartial arbitration for all sorts of disputes. AAA will provide names of real estate arbitrators in your area. I recommend you not go to any arbitration proceeding without a competent attorney representing your interests.

Index

Readers of *Crumbling Dreams* may order Dr. Martin's first book, *And They Built A Crooked House*, at a specially reduced price (see next page).

Comments about *And They Built Crooked House*:

"...details the problems a prospective home buyer can face. A well-documented, subjective report."
— The Sun Press (Cuyahoga County), August 22, 1991

"...an educational handbook for novices entering the tangled web of lawyers, lawsuits and liars."
— The Chagrin Valley Times, August 29, 1991

"...she succeeds in maintaining an admirable degree of suspense. The story soon evolves from a cautionary kvetch about shoddy construction into a compelling drama of litigation angst."
— Small Press Journal, Fall 1991

"An incredible but not uncommon story...It should be required reading for those considering the average person's largest single purchase, a new home."
— OHIOANA QUARTERLY, December 1991

"Lays out the entire wretched affair, with detailed accounts of conversations, the full text of letters and legal reports, and a blow-by-blow account of the resulting trial."
— The Raleigh News and Observer, December 15, 1991

"Might be subtitled "How Not To Hire A Contractor." Details what went wrong [and shows how] it could have been avoided."
— The Cleveland Plain Dealer, April 5, 1992

"For home-buyers it provides a clear warning: Check our your builder and get a solid contract that protects you. For home builders, it also provides a lesson: This is no way to run a business."
— The Charlotte Observer, April 18, 1992

Section 1 of *Crumbling Dreams* is a synopsis of *And They Built A Crooked House*, Dr. Martin's complete account about litigation over her defective new house (see page 7, and also comments on page 171). *Crooked House* was published in 1991 at $12.95 (paperback). Readers of *Crumbling Dreams* who wish to read the complete story of the Martins' saga, including many of the court documents, experts' reports and letters, may order *Crooked House* at less than half-price: $5.00, plus $2.50 for postage and handling (please allow a few weeks for delivery). To obtain *Crooked House* at this price please send a check or money order for $7.50 to

CROOKED HOUSE Special Offer
c/o Lakeside Press
5124 Mayfield Road, # 191
Cleveland, Ohio 44124

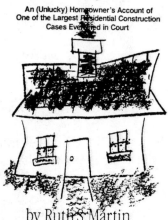

And They Built A Crooked House

An (Unlucky) Homeowner's Account of One of the Largest Residential Construction Cases Ever Tried in Court

by Ruth S. Martin

PLUS: How to Protect Yourself and Avoid a Legal Nightmare When Building or Buying a New Home